D0343015

ROLLING STONES

THE STORIES BEHIND THE BIGGEST SONGS

Steve Appleford

THIS IS A CARLTON BOOK

First published in Great Britain by
Carlton Books Limited 2010
20 Mortimer Street
London W1T 3JW

Text copyright © 1997 Steve Appleford
Design copyright © 2010 Carlton Books Limited

A CIP catalogue for this book is available from the
British Library.

ISBN 978-1-84732-695-9

Printed in China

CONTENTS

INTRODUCTION

The Thames ain't the Mississippi. And yet the blues descended on post-war London town like a prophetic message from another world – a place of moonshine, sharecroppers and bad, bad love. It was a sound fuelled by tragedy and inner strength. And it was played by men like Muddy Waters, who arrived at his first ever field recording session in July 1942 in bare feet and with a borrowed guitar, singing with profound sexual tension of getting no satisfaction at all. "I woke up this mornin', found my little baby gone."

The blues told the story of Black America, where the great singer Bessie Smith, the celebrated "Empress of the Blues", bled to death when she was denied entry into a white hospital after a car accident. It was a world where Waters (born McKinley Morganfield) was a field worker by the age of 10, making less than 75 cents a day; and where even a blues titan like the dignified Son House, the man who taught Robert Johnson himself, was caught under the indifferent thumb of a white boss and landowner.

In the early 1960s, their music of intense joy and pain made an unlikely connection with British youth, with the likes of Brian Jones and Mick Jagger and Keith Richards, who knew little of the trouble Waters had seen, but who understood that the folk blues of Mississippi was about something real and passionate.

Baby Mick had first heard those sounds as a 12-year-old, spinning race records mailed direct from America. Then in 1960, Jagger was travelling to his classes at the London School of Economics, carrying a precious stack of new vinyl by Chuck Berry, Little Walter, Muddy Waters and Mississippi Fred McDowell, when he was spotted on the train by Keith Richards. Both of these solidly middle-class urchins were born in Dartford in 1943, and had known each other as children at Wentworth County Primary School before losing touch after the age of 11. Now young Mr Richards was hungrily eyeing the records under Mick's arm: "You're into Chuck Berry, man, REALLY?"

MICK JAGGER   CHARLIE WATTS   BRIAN JONES   KEITH RICHARD   BILL WYMAN

HIT OR MISS?
THE STONES PASS
JUDGEMENT ON TV'S
JUKE BOX JURY.

Records were still a scarce luxury in those days, so Keith invited Mick up to tea. Together they studied every groove, every ragged moment of love, hate, desperation and euphoria. For Richards, the discovery of these three-minute dispatches transformed his black and white life in suburban London into glorious Technicolor. By this time, Keith had become an art school misfit, now more obsessed with learning guitar than any of his class work. Mick was already singing Buddy Holly tunes for his own amusement at weekends, and soon began jamming rock and blues tunes with Richards at a friend's house.

Mick and Keith dreamt of the monumental sounds they might make together, and often travelled to hear live music at local clubs. In 1962, they arrived at the Marquee Club in London in time to see Alexis Korner's Blues Incorporated, where they discovered a young blond guitarist sitting in, hunched like a madman over his instrument, playing slide guitar on 'Dust My Broom' not unlike the great Elmore James. Except that this cat – who called himself Elmo Lewis – wasn't from the Mississippi Delta country, but had come all the way from genteel Cheltenham for his few moments of blues glory. His real name was Brian Jones, and he told Jagger and Richards of his plans to form his own blues unit, once he escaped to London.

Jones was fanatical in his quest to create the Rollin' Stones, a name taken from a Muddy Waters lyric. And he had soon recruited Jagger, Richards, bassist Bill Wyman (nee Perks), drummer Charlie Watts (another Blues Incorporated veteran) and pianist Ian Stewart. This was Brian Jones' band. Mick was just the singer then, Keith just another guitarist. But they all shared a deep love for the rock and blues of Mississippi and Chicago, from the likes of Jimmy Reed, T-Bone Walker, Big Bill Broonzy, Bo Diddley, John Lee Hooker and dozens of other American artists largely overlooked in their own country.

The Rollin' Stones quickly found themselves at the forefront of a new movement of young British blues players, committed to spreading the gospel according to Chess Records, home to many of the most distinctive bluesmen and rockers. It was an almost religious experience for the pious Stones, copying the old blues standards as if they were scripture, never pausing to seriously consider writing their own material as the Beatles had done from the very beginning. Anything else would have been SACRILEGE, or at least require an effort thus far beyond the band's reach. What could these London choirboys have to offer that hadn't already been said to greater effect by the original blues masters?

Jagger's voice was not yet the distinctive, seething growl that would emerge in the coming years, and was sometimes lost amidst the earnestness of the band's delivery. Likewise, Jones and Richards were hardly instrumental virtuosos, not in the manner that would have overheated graffiti artists declaring Eric Clapton as God. The duo instead locked together into a tight rhythmic juggernaut, working toward a rare mastery of rhythm guitar, the core element that would lead to the mature Stones sound later heard within 'Brown Sugar' and Exile On Main Street.

Soon, the Stones were joined on the stages of London by a crowd of new blues-based artists in search of their own musical voices. The Animals arrived from Newcastle. Spencer Davis and Stevie Winwood came from Birmingham. Any new band hoping to succeed had to come to London. "It was a fresh thing for most people because for ten years people had been listening to nothing but New Orleans jazz, then called Trad Jazz," says John Mayall, who arrived from Manchester in 1963, leaving his job in the graphics department of a hometown advertizing agency. "That had been the reigning music in all the clubs. That same lineup of trumpet, trombone, clarinet and the rhythm section was all people really heard until this fresh Chicago sound came in. It appealed to the young generation. They'd had an audience in the coffee shops and the folk clubs at that time in London. They just took it a step further. They were heavily influenced by Muddy Waters' work with Little Walter and the amplifiers and so forth – they just got electrified. And in those same folk clubs they started to get an audience."

At the centre of that movement was Alexis Korner, whose Blues Incorporated launched the careers of many young blues players. He also arranged for the Stones to share bills with visiting American bluesmen. If Korner was not one of the scene's exceptional guitarists, his great enthusiasm for fellow players inspired many. Mayall remembers Korner's constant encouragement, and how the Hungarian-born guitarist personally

"WE'RE THE ONLY BAND TO MAKE IT THIS FAR, AND IF WE TRIP AND FALL YOU'LL KNOW THAT'S HOW FAR IT CAN BE TAKEN."
KEITH RICHARDS

introduced Mayall to London club-owners and musicians, essentially kick-starting Mayall's career as bandleader to the Bluesbreakers.

"It was Alexis' movement," recalls Mick Farren, a musician and writer who would later make his mark with the Deviants. "He was a great proselytizer. He was a really lovely guy. If he had it, he'd lend you money, and listen to your problems. He was everybody's godfather, rabbi, whatever. Alexis was an exceptional guy."

Among the young blues acts travelling the back roads of England with visiting American bluesmen was Chicken Shack, a band that included singer and pianist Christine McVie (née Perfect), later of Fleetwood Mac. "We used to have B.B. King and Freddie Guy and all these characters come over from the States, and all these white English groups would support them and go on pub tours with them," McVie remembers fondly. "American blues became such a part of the English subculture back then. People were hunting around for these obscure 45 singles. It was wonderful."

Soon enough, the traditional jazz bands were being elbowed aside in London clubs to make room for increasingly popular British blues bands. "Brian was so pleased to see the last jazz band disband and us taking over the clubs," Richards told Stanley Booth in Dancing With the Devil/The True Adventures Of The Rolling Stones. "It was his happiest, proudest moment."

During these first years, Jones was the prime mover behind the Rollin' Stones. Playing the blues was now his life. He had been kicked out of college, drifted from one job to another, and he already fathered at least one son. Mick and Keith were still living at home, far from being the great hedonists the Glimmer Twins would later become. "Success never came into it," Richards told Creem magazine in 1975. "We never dreamed of it, never even thought we could turn the whole of London on to what we were doing, let alone the world. We didn't even think like that. We just thought, 'wouldn't it be great if we could play one night a week with a few people dancing?'"

There was a growing authenticity in the Stones' delivery of these R&B experiments. "I thought it came off real," says Bobby Womack, co-author of 'It's All Over Now', which became the Stones' first UK chart-topper in 1964. "It was them being real with what they were about. Sometimes you can't be somebody else. You're going to be yourself, no matter what they do. So they put their English touch into it, and they introduced to white audiences all around the world how important singing from the heart and singing soul was. That caused the black music to be recognized. Think about it: B.B. King had been kicking for years, Tina Turner, a lot of artists.

ROLLING ON: THE STONES IN THE 1970S. WHO WOULD HAVE THOUGHT THEY WOULD STILL BE ON THE ROAD ALMOST A HALF A CENTURY AFTER THEY FIRST FORMED?

The Rolling Stones said it was OK to feel this music. Forget the politics. Music ain't about that. It made the music grow."

Rock and roll was also always part of the Stones' mix, guaranteed by the presence of Richards, who worshipped the flying riffs and wry minimalist poetry of Chuck Berry at least as much as the heavy blues of Muddy Waters. That meant poor Brian had to endure the occasional Chuck Berry rocker during their sets, never imagining that the Stones legacy would hinge less on blues devotion than to recreating rock and roll in their own image.

In March 1963, the Stones caught the attention of Andrew Loog Oldham, hipster impressario and a former publicist for the Beatles. He convinced the band he should be their manager, and had them in a studio a week later to record Chuck Berry's 'Come On', the band's first single. His influence was dramatic. First, he convinced Jones to drop founding pianist Ian Stewart from the band, simply because he looked too square. He put the remaining quintet in matching suits with black velvet collars – like the Beatles – but quickly played up the bad-boy angle, ruining their reputations for good citizenship for the sake of newspaper headlines. Most profoundly, Oldham demanded that Jagger and Richards begin writing original material, a career move that made their continued survival possible.

If Oldham tended to guide the Rolling Stones with the most commercial pop aims in mind, the band never abandoned their love for American R&B. During their first tour of the United States, they immediately sought out the famed Harlem Apollo, where they watched Joe Tex, Wilson Picket and James Brown demonstrate the state of their art.

"We wanted to be a blues band, but then we gave it up because it was a complete waste of time," Jagger told *Creem* in 1978. "Keith kept saying we're a *blues* band. I didn't give a shit what they wanted to call it in the end. In the beginning we were very dedicated. We didn't want to be called a *rock* band. So we did something else 'cause we couldn't do R&B exactly right. And because we couldn't do it exactly the same way, we HAD to do it our own way."

The Stones sound had already changed by the time Lennon and McCartney offered them 'I Wanna Be Your Man'. In the Stones' hands, the song was more primal, more seething than the cleaned-up version later done by the Fab Four. The song was their big break on to the charts, but their greatest successes came only when the band stepped out of the purism that hobbled the earliest days of their contemporaries, and sought a new, darker voice. The hard-headed boogie-woogie absolutism of Ian Stewart would never have lasted in a world of 'Let It Bleed' and 'Wild Horses'.

"The Rolling Stones, starting with that blues base, they brought it up into a more modern sonic dimension," says guitarist Wayne Kramer of the MC5. "They started using the sounds that you can get out of electric guitars, and really finding the core of the power of that sound and those tones you can get from overdriving an amplifier a little bit. Some of the those songs were brilliant, masterful productions."

For their followers, every new Stones single, every new batch of tracks, were like a dispatch to the world. And more often than not during the 1960s, the Stones built on their history, singing and playing to ever greater effect on love, hate, faith, decadence, addiction and fame. For the MC5, those messages emerged with a harsh clarity. While on tour in the summer of 1969, the MC5 were travelling along some long-forgotten expressway when the radio DJ announced that he had the new Stones single, something called 'Honky Tonk Women'. "We cranked it up, and it just floored us all," Kramer remembers. "We just said, 'Man, the Stones did it again! Man, they did it, man! LISTEN TO THAT SHIT, MAN!!! THEY'RE FUCKING NAILING IT!!!' It was like winning the pennant: the beat, the guitar tone, the solo, the whole thing was brilliant."

By the 1970s, the Stones were calling themselves "The World's Greatest Rock And Roll Band". Newer acts like Led Zeppelin were already surpassing them in gross sales, but the Stones' history and influence could not be eclipsed. More than three decades later, the Stones remain. Along the way, Brian Jones was found dead, Bill Wyman became a retired, elderly restauranteur, Mick Taylor walked away from the best and worst gig in rock, a bored Mick Jagger had a diamond embedded into his tooth, and Keith Richards continued a never-ending search for that perfect riff.

9

THE ROLLING STONES

Recorded	January to February 1964, Regent Sound Studios, London.
Produced by	Eric Easton and Andrew Loog Oldham.
Musicians	The Rolling Stones: Mick Jagger (vocals, harmonica, percussion), Brian Jones (guitar, harmonica, percussion, backing vocals), Keith Richards (guitar, backing vocals), Charlie Watts (drums, percussion), Bill Wyman (bass guitar, backing vocals). Additional musicians: Gene Pitney (piano), Phil Spector (maracas), Ian Stewart (organ and piano).

ROUTE 66 (TROUP)

I JUST WANT TO MAKE LOVE TO YOU (DIXON)

HONEST I DO (REED)

I NEED YOU BABY (MCDANIELS)

NOW I'VE GOT A WITNESS
   (LIKE UNCLE PHIL AND UNCLE GENE) (PHELGE)

LITTLE BY LITTLE (PHELGE/SPECTOR)

I'M A KING BEE (MOORE)

CAROL (BERRY)

TELL ME (YOU'RE COMING BACK)

CAN I GET A WITNESS (HOLLAND/DOZIER/HOLLAND)

YOU CAN MAKE IT IF YOU TRY (JARRETT)

WALKING THE DOG (THOMAS)

11

Pity the young Rollin' Stones, trying so hard to get it right. Their love of the blues was real. Their commitment to the sound of Black America boundless, thanks largely to the fanaticism of little Brian Jones. Such innocence, and so worshipful of the great bluesmen of Chicago and the Deep South. And yet in the context of Britain in 1964 – a nation afloat on good vibes from the happy, shiny Beatles – these brooding boys from London looked like very bad news indeed.

But what were they really? *Thieves* stealing the very soul of American R&B, little better than Pat Boone crooning whitebread renditions of Little

MICK JAGGER AND ANDREW LOOG OLDHAM, THE BAND'S MANAGER.

Richard and Fats Domino tunes, helping to keep the segregated pop charts clean and bright. The difference, of course, was that the Stones at least seemed to understand the music they were playing, digging those crazy sounds for all they were worth.

Not that the Stones were out to clean up the blues. In their hands, it remained a potent force, a sound virtually unknown to polite middle-class England. They just wanted to be young R&B prophets, spreading the good news of the deeply passionate music of Muddy Waters, Elmore James and Howlin' Wolf. Pop wasn't their mission. At least not yet, even if manager Andrew Loog Oldham already had other ideas. His plan was to sell his Fab Five as the anti-Beatles, a quintet of surly bad boys ready to wreak havoc on society and its daughters. Their evil intent was quickly established with Oldham's well-publicized question: "Would you let your daughter marry a Rolling Stone?"

The answer seemed clear enough in the messages of seething manhood found within songs like Slim Harpo's 'I'm a King Bee' – "I can make honey, baby, let me come inside" – and revelations that Brian had already fathered two children by two separate lady friends.

Maybe the Rolling Stones just wanted to play their blues and rock and roll, but Oldham had noticed the beginning of Beatlemania in America just a few months earlier. It was clear that a British Invasion of the US was brewing, and he wanted the Stones to be part of it. Thus the Rolling Stones' eponymous debut album would be better known to Americans by its subtitle, *England's Newest Hitmakers* – surely an indication of just which bandwagon Jagger and his cohorts were boarding. And yet a look at the track listing of The Rolling Stones shows a band still smitten with their beloved R&B and Chuck Berry-style rock, not a group of hooligans out to cash in on the next big pop thing.

"Being pop stars didn't even come into the realm of possibility," Keith Richards told journalist Lisa Robinson in 1989. "We saw no connection between us and the Beatles – we were playing blues, they were writing pop songs dressed in suits. We were too hip to be pop stars, it was like that was the only dignity we had left."

Their first single, released in the summer of 1963, had put the band's shared interests to work on Chuck Berry's 'Come On' and Willie Dixon's 'I Want To Be Loved'. It was a modest success, hitting No. 21 on the UK singles chart. The Stones pattern in those early days was to find worthy R&B songs that were virtually unknown in England, and had been unreasonably ignored back in the US. That formula took The Rolling Stones to the top of the UK album chart for 11 weeks, while reaching No. 11 in the US. Two months later, the Stones earned their first chart-topping single with a cover of the Valentinos' 'It's All Over Now'. This wasn't exactly welcome news to co-author Bobby Womack. He and his brothers in the Valentinos were an American R&B band struggling to cross over to lucrative white audiences, and just beginning to enjoy some success with 'It's All Over Now'. Soulman Sam Cooke, who signed the Valentinos to his Sar Records label, warned Womack about the upcoming version of his song by the Stones, and suggested that it could be a good thing.

"I was very angry about it," says Womack now. "That was the first song that I had written that became a big record and was going real big for me and my brothers. That's hard to understand when you come from the ghetto and you finally get a record and you know the importance of it. I knew their record was going to go so far, and ours was going to quit."

But Cooke turned out to be completely right, says Womack, now a longtime friend and occasional sideman to the Stones. "The record immediately took off and it carried us a long way. When I saw the first cheque I was shocked. It was huge." The song's success was a boost to Womack's career, and he has continued to receive fat royalty cheques ever since. "I said to the Stones after we met, 'I've been chasing you guys to get you to record another song.'"

Sessions for The Rolling Stones began in late January 1964 at Regent Sound in London. The Stones were by now a tight, toughened unit, fresh from their first major UK tour with the Everly Brothers, Bo Diddley and the Ronnettes. But Jagger was still a boy, singing Willie Dixon's 'I Just Want To Make Love To You' more like a sloppy kid than with the fire and dread of a Muddy Waters. His voice was often thin, and uncertain during those first album sessions. The blues were not yet his own. But even as the Stones watered down the blues of Jimmy Reed's 'Honest I Do', their performance still carried an element of danger.

The album was produced on a simple two-track machine by the multi-talented Andrew Loog Oldham, who in fact had absolutely no experience in the studio at that time. He had thought that electric guitars were plugged directly into wall sockets and (fortunately for the band) that the final mixing of the tapes was a boring inconvenience best left to the lowly sound engineer. Oldham largely stepped back and allowed for the simple documentation of the Stones sound: the clashing guitars, the euphoric moaning of harmonica, the rollicking keyboard work of the banished Ian Stewart. The result was an album of raw, primal force, pushing classic R&B toward the edgy rock terrain that the Stones would soon come to epitomize.

Oldham's main contribution to the Stones was his insistence that the band should begin writing original material. He was rightly convinced that the group's future would be limited if it depended on searching out obscure R&B gems to cover. Jagger and Richards knew it could be done. They had seen it with their own eyes the previous September when Lennon and McCartney visited their rehearsal space in Soho. The Beatle composers had been working on a song called 'I Wanna Be Your Man' for Ringo, but it was unfinished. As Jagger and Richards watched, the dynamic duo completed the song and offered it to the Stones. Within a month, the supercharged 'I Wanna Be Your Man' had become the Rolling Stones' first top-10 single.

"We thought it sounded pretty commercial, which is what we were looking for, so we did it like Elmore James or something," Jagger told Rolling Stone in 1968. "I haven't heard it for ages but it must be pretty freaky 'cause nobody really produced it... but it was a hit and sounded great on stage."

One day, Oldham pushed Jagger and Richards into a room with instructions not to leave until they had written at least one song. And that's what they did. So three songs on The Rolling Stones were credited to either the mysterious Nanker Phelge – a nonsensical *nom de plume* for group compositions – or to Jagger and Richards. The Glimmer Twins were born.

NOW I'VE GOT A WITNESS (LIKE UNCLE PHIL AND UNCLE GENE)

Motown gone wrong. This light-hearted instrumental jam was the first original song to appear on a Rolling Stones album. Credited to Nanker Phelge, the track rides a soft blues rhythm that emerged during their session covering the Marvin Gaye hit 'Can I Get a Witness'. 'Now I've Got A Witness' borrows the same central keyboard riff, replacing the revival-meeting piano melody with a swell of organ. Wistful blues harp cuts across Charlie Watts' rock steady beat before the track finally catches fire with a charged Keith guitar lead.

"BEING POP STARS DIDN'T EVEN COME INTO THE REALM OF POSSIBILITY."
KEITH RICHARDS

Nothing profound about their performance, just joyful playing. The Uncles Phil and Gene in the title refer to producer Phil Spector and pop singer Gene Pitney, who were frequent visitors to the sessions for The Rolling Stones. Spector was the mad studio genius whose "wall of sound" created a rich musical fabric for 1960s pop epics by the likes of the Crystals and the Ronnettes. His studio magic made for some visionary pop, although not exactly relevant to the blues and rock of the Stones. Spector's presence at Regent Sound was just for friendly encouragement and to keep a wary eye on his sexpot wife, singer Ronnie Spector, who had just met the Stones while touring England. Crooner Pitney had often collaborated with Spector, crafting weepy epics memorable for their rich melodramatic arrangements. Though a songwriter himself – he had written 'Hello Mary Lou' for Ricky Nelson – Pitney scored another hit in January 1964 with the early Jagger/Richards song 'That Girl Belongs To Yesterday'. It was the first Glimmer Twins composition to hit the US charts.

'Now I've Got A Witness' was perhaps most notable for its clear view of the young players in the Rolling Stones. Uncluttered by Jagger's mush-mouthed approximation of the blues, the track captured the legendary rhythm section in its earliest glory.

"Bill and Charlie locked together," notes Bobby Womack, who would later witness the Stones at work many times on stage and in the studio. "Bill made Charlie a hell of a drummer, and vice versa – he made him a hell of a bass player. Being a musician is not how many notes you play, but what you don't play. Music is simplicity."

LITTLE BY LITTLE

Bad love is as timeless as the blues itself. It's sent men no less formidable than Willie Dixon, Muddy Waters and B.B. King into howls of joy and hate, crafting soul-searching music as mournful as it is strangely euphoric. Love gone wrong also provided the young Stones with an early successful attempt at blues authenticity.

'Little By Little' mixes a young man's pain and resignation with a frenetic blues-rock rhythm as foreboding as the album's shadowy cover photograph of five grim-faced young men, solemnly preparing for some unspeakably dirty work.

Co-credited to Nanker Phelge and Phil Spector, 'Little By Little' made its debut as the B-side to their hit single of Buddy Holly's 'Not Fade Away' (which was included on the US version of the album). While Spector plays maracas, Jagger portrays a man stalking his woman, watching from his car, afraid of the heartbreak he expects to find as he follows her to some unknown rendezvous.

Between flashes of harmonica, Jagger sings more about internal pain than the more suggestive contents of the blues originals featured on the album. He might as well have been a heartbroken teenager – he was still only 19 at the time of this session on February 4, 1964. And yet Jagger finds new depth within his voice, a grinding edge that would emerge as a key element in the classic Stones sound, finally turning the black man's rhythm and blues into something of his own.

"Nobody sounds like Mick," says Bobby Womack. "You can say you know artists that are much better, but if I tried to sing like Mick I would be totally out of his league. When you're different, it's like Ray Charles. He's a stylist."

TELL ME
(YOU'RE COMING BACK)

This was a long way from the music the Stones had initially set out to play. But 'Tell Me (You're Coming Back To Me)' was an early indication that the new Jagger/Richards writing team was capable of crafting a song worthy of the band's time. It was only a first step for the Glimmer Twins, but the

PHIL SPECTOR CAME ALONG TO THE STUDIO TO LEND A HAND... AND TO KEEP AN EYE ON HIS WIFE RONNIE, WHO HAD RECENTLY BECOME FRIENDLY WITH THE STONES.

song's pleasant, if unspectacular, pop melody was a move toward undermining the dominance of Brian Jones.

Keith plays a jangly 12-string guitar and sings harmonies into the same microphone, as Jagger's vocals fall just short of pleading.

"It's a very *pop* song, as opposed to all the blues songs and the Motown covers, which everyone did at the time," Mick Jagger told *Rolling Stone* magazine in 1995.

Other new compositions that emerged at the same time included 'As Tears Go By' and 'That Girl Belongs To Yesterday'. They had little in common with the blues, or with the bare-knuckle rock the Stones would later create, but this early balladry was an important foundation for the melodic pop of their dynamic work of the mid-sixties.

"We were writing ballads – don't ask me why," Jagger said. "We didn't want to do blues forever, we just wanted to turn people on to other people who were very good and not carry on doing it ourselves," Jagger explained later. "So you could say that we did turn blues on to people, but why they should be turned on by us is unbelievably stupid. I mean, what's the point of listening to us doing 'I'm A King Bee' when you could listen to Slim Harpo doing it?"

ROLLING STONES NO. 2

Recorded	June, September, November 1964, Chess Studios, Chicago, Illinois; RCA Studios, Hollywood, California, Regent Sound Studios, London.
Produced by	Andrew Loog Oldham.
Musicians	The Rolling Stones: Mick Jagger (vocals, harmonica, tambourine, percussion), Brian Jones (guitar, slide guitar, backing vocals), Keith Richards (guitar, backing vocals), Charlie Watts (drums, percussion), Bill Wyman (bass guitar, backing vocals). Additional musicians: Jack Nitzsche (piano, 'Nitzsche' phone, tambourine), Ian Stewart (piano).

EVERYBODY NEEDS SOMEBODY TO LOVE (RUSSELL/BURKE/WEXLER)
DOWN HOME GIRL (LEIBER/BUTLER)
YOU CAN'T CATCH ME (BERRY)
TIME IS ON MY SIDE (MEADE/NORMAN)
WHAT A SHAME
GROWN UP WRONG
DOWN THE ROAD APIECE (RAYE)
UNDER THE BOARDWALK (RESNICK/YOUNG)
I CAN'T BE SATISFIED (WATERS)
PAIN IN MY HEART (REDDING/WALDEN)
OFF THE HOOK
SUZIE Q (BROADWATER/LEWIS/HAWKINS)

THE YOUNG MICK JAGGER, LIGHTING A FUSE THAT WOULD DRIVE THE YOUNG GIRLS WILD.

Let the rioting begin. Maybe Andrew Oldham was a genius after all, selling the Rolling Stones as a pack of dangerous delinquents. It was driving the little girls mad, and had sent The Rolling Stones album to the top of the UK chart for 11 impossible weeks. Until then, their shows across Britain had taken place with little incident – just the occasional sad-eyed girl looking for idols. Now there were 4,000 gate-crashers with phony tickets rioting outside their performance in Aberdeen. And soon the halls of Europe would be aflame with the passion of teens erupting to the sounds of blues and soul, sending chairs and chandelier pieces through the air, with girls being carried out in straight jackets, boys spitting at Brian and Keith, ripping the clothes off young women. And police everywhere, hopelessly addled and confused.

This was the Stones legacy of 1964. And yet the master of this great rock and roll swindle was young Andrew – every bit to the early Rolling Stones what Malcolm McLaren would be to the Sex Pistols in 1976. He was not there to create, but to exploit. Both were impresarios in search of the worst publicity imaginable – taking any opportunity to create an alarming headline. Oldham also fancied himself as a producer in the epic Phil Spector mould, arriving at the studio in dark threads and shades. He even wrote liner notes to the albums in the cryptic hipster-speak of Anthony Burgess' novel *A Clockwork Orange* – "Here are your new groovies so please a-bound to the sound". Mick Farren, writer and leader of the Deviants recalled: "He was like a beatnik, but a few years too late."

So the rioting rolled on. The Stones set out on a three-week tour of the US. It was the beginning of three years of almost constant travel and performing, a lifestyle that would have a profound effect on the frail Brian Jones.

As it turned out, there was little rioting in the United States. The Stones had perhaps come too early, unlike the Beatles, who waited until 'I Want To Hold Your Hand' was a No. 1 hit in America before landing at Kennedy Airport to a greeting from thousands of screaming fans and Mr Ed Sullivan.

Despite Andrew's evil brainstorming, the Stones' career was never quite so premeditated. If the Beatles seemed to live in a rock and roll fairy tale, the Rolling Stones' biography would never read quite so smoothly. In any case, why should the Stones have waited any longer? After all, as the 500 fans who greeted them well understood, these were indeed "ENGLAND'S NEWEST HITMAKERS!"

The first Rolling Stones tour of the US – along with Bobby Vee, the Chiffons, Bobby Goldsboro and Bobby Comstock – did very well on the coasts, hitting New York and Los Angeles like visiting pop royalty. But the band had a tougher time travelling the great expanse of emptiness in between, enduring small crowds and Midwestern ambivalence. Even before the tour officially began, the Rolling Stones found themselves, their sound and their dress, the subject of ridicule.

In the days leading up to their first gig in nearby San Bernardino, the band appeared at a Los Angeles taping of Dean Martin's Hollywood Palace Show. Here they were seen on American television playing Willie Dixon's shuddering 'I Just Want To Make Love To You', Brian beneath his great helmet of yellow-blond hair, Keith twitching nervously through his riffs, Bill holding his bass like a shotgun, Mick clapping and kicking his heels politely and Charlie somehow oblivious on the drum seat and looking the most comfortable in his own skin. But Dino didn't much like their hair or their music. And he certainly didn't understand the blues – "Now something for the youngsters…"

Dino was a hipster from the old school, a wisecracking, crooning funnyman in greased hair, forever carrying a burning cigarette in one hand, a tumbler of booze in the other. He was a product of the World War II generation, whose cultural dominance was most threatened by the likes of the Beatles and the Stones. Even Elvis was worried.

"Some people have the impression that some of these new groups have long hair," Martin told the Palace audience with a roll of his eyes. "Naaaaaaaaah, it's an optical illusion, they just have low foreheads and high eyebrows." Their parents, Dino went on, had even contemplated suicide at the very idea of the Stones and their music.

Insulting? Yes, but by the time the show was broadcast across the nation ten days later, it hardly mattered at all. The Stones had arrived at Chess Studios in Chicago, the "Holy Grail" of American blues and rock and roll, and the site of immortal recordings by Muddy Waters, Chuck Berry, Little Walter and Bo Diddley. While they were there, the band recorded 'It's All Over Now', 'Confessin' The Blues' and '2120 Michigan Avenue',

"WE WERE BLUES PURISTS WHO LIKED EVER SO COMMERCIAL THINGS BUT NEVER DID THEM ON STAGE BECAUSE WE WERE SO HORRIBLE AND SO AWARE OF BEING BLUES PURISTS… YOU KNOW WHAT I MEAN?" MICK JAGGER

encouraged by the masters – Chuck and Muddy – who visited the Stones sessions to see these young white R&B fanatics for themselves.

The early 1960s had been lean years for the Chess roster, and the Rolling Stones were bringing their music back into the spotlight. For years, Richards claimed that when the Stones arrived at Chess, they found Waters at work painting the ceiling, though Wyman disputes the memory. Either way, bands like the Stones and, later, the Yardbirds and the Animals, were helping to keep the music alive for a new generation.

Yet as each of those acts would quickly demonstrate, the irresistible attraction of POP was as real as the latest Beatles chart triumph. The Stones managed without trouble to stay true to their roots while recording within the hallowed halls of Chess, but it was just as inevitable that a change was gonna come. As Jagger explained to Rolling Stone in 1995, "We were blues purists who liked ever so commercial things but never did them on stage because we were so horrible and so aware of being blues purists... you know what I mean?"

On their return to England, the Stones found that local hysteria had only intensified in their absence. A concert in Belfast was halted after just 12 minutes as police grew increasingly alarmed at the sight of fainting girls and shouting boys. In Paris, more than 150 fans were arrested during rioting at the Olympia. It was the kind of bad press Andrew had fantasized about. Now the Stones found themselves banned from hotels and refused service in the best restaurants. His dream had come true.

What was behind all of this? The authorities only had to look at the Stones album covers to realize their worst fears. As on their debut, the sleeve of *The Rolling Stones No. 2* – photographed by David Bailey – presented the band as a gang of brooding young thugs. The music inside was dark and rumbling. It had been recorded during the band's second tour of the US at the end of 1964, shortly after Charlie's wedding to Shirley Ann Shepherd. If the first album owed its raw edge to the barebones setting of Regent Sound, *The Rolling Stones No. 2* found a new potency within the studios of Chess and RCA in Hollywood, home of Elvis Presley. "It is very soul influenced, which was the goal at the time – Otis Redding and Solomon Burke," Jagger said later of the album.

An immediate success, the new album entered the British chart at No. 1, turning the Rolling Stones into instant rivals for the Beatles' pop crown. In truth, however, *The Rolling Stones No. 2* was less impressive as a musical document. None of the three original compositions here were particularly memorable, and were easily overshadowed by the band's

recording of 'Time Is On My Side'. Though faithful to the Irma Thomas original, the Rolling Stones made the song their own with Jagger's heartfelt reading and Richards' most dynamic guitar work to date. Also included was an unfortunate attempt by Jagger to recreate the wistful romance of 'Under The Boardwalk'. But even amidst the erratic mix of hits and missteps, the Rolling Stones were slowly refining their role, and laying a foundation for the important work to come.

WHAT A SHAME

First released in December 1964 as the B-side to the Jagger/Richards-penned single 'Heart Of Stone', 'What A Shame' reveals the Stones confidently creating some blues of their own. Jagger's pipes are deeper, gliding across searing blasts of harmonica, the spirited piano riffs of Ian Stewart at the edges, and the Wyman-Watts rhythm section snapping it all into place. By the time a lengthy instrumental jam closes the track, the Rolling Stones have nearly mastered a form they first encountered as boys studying Chess imports from America.

That confidence doesn't emerge everywhere on *The Rolling Stones No. 2*, but 'What A Shame' at least documents the Stones in command of a basic blues formula – nothing fancy, and nothing that Brian Jones hadn't already preached as the one true path. Jagger and Richards had – with the encouragement of their manager – now claimed for themselves the task of writing original material for the band. The sharing of songwriting credits as "Nanker Phelge" was now a thing of the past. The reality in 1965, though, was that the defining vision for the band had not yet been relinquished by the fanatical Elmo Lewis.

"The Rolling Stones that I joined were led by Brian Jones," Bill Wyman wrote in his autobiography, *Stone Alone*. "To the millions who figured it was Mick Jagger's band, it may come as a shock to record that in 1963 Mick was simply the singer. There was no doubt whatsoever who led the group in every way. Brian called the shots partly because he had pulled the musicians together, but mainly because what mattered most at that stage was music, and Brian was by far the most knowledgeable about what we were playing."

Jones would never be able to compete with the developing songwriting talents of Mick Jagger and Keith Richards, but he remained a key player in the sound of the Stones until creeping bad habits, failing health and paranoia slowly took it all away. His collapse in Chicago from physical exhaustion while on tour was an early signal that Jones might be unable to keep up with his creation.

GROWN UP WRONG

The Stones roadshow now rolled ever onward. During their second American tour, the band debuted on the influential *Ed Sullivan Show* on October 25, 1964. The result was a near riot of screaming young men and women in Sullivan's studio audience, leaving the host a shaken man. "I promise you they will never be back to our show," he told the assembled press. "They were recommended by my scouts in England. I was shocked when I saw them."

Rock and roll was becoming dangerous, as seen on TV. And yet the Stones would of course be back on Sullivan's stage within a year. Sullivan had seen this kind of hysteria twice before, first with Elvis Presley, whose offending pelvic thrusts and gyrations had to be cropped from the TV picture. But Sullivan had also taken Presley in his arms during the broadcast to declare him "a fine young man". Similarly, the Beatles had also come and gone with little real trouble.

How strange that Sullivan's early anxieties of the fearsome Stones emerged from a fittingly restrained reading of 'Time Is On My Side'. If anything, Mick performed the song as a classic romantic, politely tapping his feet. Jagger hadn't yet learned to chew the scenery from his first dose of live James Brown.

Likewise, Jagger's vocal chops were not fully developed at the time of *The Rolling Stones No. 2*. He sounds earnest enough on 'Grown Up Wrong', but his vocals lack the weight of his blues and soul models. Even with the accompaniment of Jones' testy slide guitar, Jagger in 1965 simply didn't sound like someone ready to offer meaningful advice about love. That wouldn't come until the deeply moving performances of raw blues and country on 1968's *Beggars Banquet*.

In America, 'Grown Up Wrong' appears on *12 x 5*, the Stones' second album release in the US – a typical bastardization of the UK releases. Material from *The Rolling Stones No. 2* was roughly divided in the States between *12 x 5* and *The Rolling Stones Now*, both of which are filled out with miscellaneous singles and EP tracks. Although the Beatles suffered a similar fate with their early albums, discrepancies were eventually resolved with the CD reissues. The early Stones catalogue, controlled by Allen Klein's ABKCO Records, still remains something of a mess.

OFF THE HOOK

This charmingly simple pop nugget was the first Jagger/Richards composition to suggest the pure pop-rock sensibility that would emerge with such impact on 1967's *Between The Buttons*. Recorded at London's Regent Sound Studios on September 2, 1964, 'Off The Hook' first appeared just two months later as the B-side to the band's 'Little Red Rooster' single, which quickly topped the UK chart.

The song opens with a buoyant Chuck Berry-style guitar melody, as Jagger sings of calling his girlfriend late one night only to find her line constantly busy. He sounds ready to accept any explanation – she's asleep, she's ill, her line's been disconnected for an unpaid bill – except for the unmentioned possibility that she's found someone new. His tone is closer to irritation than worry, but still far from the bitter female trouble Jagger would regularly complain about in the Rolling Stones songs of the coming four decades.

THE GUITAR PLAYING OF CHUCK BERRY *(RIGHT)* HAD A PROFOUND INFLUENCE ON KEITH RICHARDS.

OUT OF OUR HEADS

Recorded	November 1964 to September 1965, Chess Studios, Chicago, Illinois; RCA Studios, Hollywood, California.
Produced by	Andrew Loog Oldham
Musicians	The Rolling Stones: Mick Jagger (vocals, harmonica, percussion), Brian Jones (electric and acoustic guitar, harmonica, organ, backing vocals), Keith Richards (guitar, backing vocals), Charlie Watts (drums, percussion), Bill Wyman (bass guitar, backing vocals). Additional musicians: Jack Nitzsche (organ, piano, percussion), Phil Spector (bass guitar), Ian Stewart (piano).

SHE SAID YEAH (JACKSON/CHRISTY)
MERCY, MERCY (COVAY/MILLER)
HITCH HIKE (GAYE/STEVENSON/PAUL)
THAT'S HOW STRONG MY LOVE IS (JAMISON)
GOOD TIMES (COOKE)
GOTTA GET AWAY
TALKIN' 'BOUT YOU (BERRY)
CRY TO ME (RUSSELL)
OH BABY (WE GOT A GOOD THING GOIN') (OZEN)
HEART OF STONE
THE UNDER ASSISTANT WEST COAST PROMOTION MAN (PHELGE)
I'M FREE

AT HOME IN AMERICA: THE STONES TAKE A CRUISE DURING A BREAK FROM THE NEVER-ENDING ROCK AND ROLL ROADSHOW.

Keith Richards had a dream, and the dream was good. Another night on the road in the States in May 1965, and Keith was jarred awake in his Florida motel bed by a sound echoing in his skull. It was a fierce rumbling, with the words "can't get no satisfaction, can't get no satisfaction" mercilessly rolling between his ears. He played it immediately using his new Gibson Fuzzbox and taped it before passing out again. What was this? Not even Keith knew, so when the Stones twice attempted '(I Can't Get No) Satisfaction' at Chess and RCA Studios that same week, he rejected the song as virtually unreleasable, at least as a single. Too damn simple, with a riff dangerously close to Martha and the Vandellas' 'Dancing In The Street'. Andrew Loog Oldham soon convinced him otherwise. 'Satisfaction' was released as a single that same month. It became the band's first American No. 1 hit. Everything had now changed – the Rolling Stones had experienced their first absolutely decisive moment.

'Satisfaction' was music designed to explode from a small transistor radio, that lo-fi conduit between pop culture and the adolescent masses. It was the sound of testosterone boiling over, Jagger demanding sexual healing, Richards' fuzzy guitar a fucking ball of nerves. No one had ever made a sound quite like this before, not Muddy or Chuck or Bo. If the implied raunch of the Stones' billion blues covers hadn't already transmitted the message, 'Satisfaction' made clear everything that parents feared for their children – SEX.

"When they assimilated the blues aspect *into* the band, that's when it really happened for me," says Ray Manzarek, keyboard player with the Doors, who had grown up hearing the blues in Chicago. Until then, he had found the British blues bands nice, but hardly definitive next to the originals. "The first time I heard 'Satisfaction' on the radio I couldn't believe it. The lyrics were so terrific, they were talking to all young American males. This guy is singing a song to *us.*"

The song had emerged from a typically harried schedule of recording sessions, squeezed between concert dates: four tracks recorded in 17 hours at Chess in Chicago, followed immediately by three more tracks in two days at RCA in Hollywood. The result was *Out Of Our Heads*, which, like the 'Satisfaction' single, was first released in the US in July. This, rather ironically, made it the original version of the album, which had a significantly different, and diminished, track listing by the time it was released in the UK that September.

"I think it was because we were actually there," Andrew Oldham told journalist Craig Rosen in 1994, discussing the band's decision to release the album in the States first. "Once you make a record like 'Satisfaction' you basically just want to get it out. We weren't going to be back in England for quite a while, and you really couldn't put something out in England without being there. It was something you just don't do. It really would have been slighting people."

The Rolling Stones were rarely home now, except as another stop on their endless world tour. There were the occasional pit stops in England, long enough to find a new pad, buy a sports car or be fitted for a fur parka. Then it was back on the road. They were enjoying their accelerating success, even with the usual mishaps along the way. One afternoon in Odense, Denmark, Jagger was nearly fried from an electrical shock during rehearsals. Later, some 3,000 Australians rioted upon their arrival at the Sydney airport, and 40 fans charged the stage in Brisbane, ripping the clothes off whatever Stones they could reach. And back in the UK, a Manchester girl broke some teeth after falling from a balcony during a show.

Then, at the end of a UK tour, the Rolling Stones had their first brush with the law, an early warning of the strange days to come. The Stones were returning to London on March 18, 1965, when Ian Stewart pulled the car over at a filling station in East London. There, Wyman was denied use of the toilet by a cheeky mechanic named Charles Keely, who later referred to the Stones as "long-haired monsters". Wyman, Jones and Jagger then decided to use a nearby wall instead, shouted a few insults at Keely and drove off. The incident was immediately reported in the press, and the Stones were charged with insulting behaviour by urinating in public. They were each fined £5 in July. The judge told them: "Because you have reached the exalted heights in your profession, it does not mean you have the right to act like this… You have been found guilty of behaviour not becoming young gentlemen."

Travelling across the US was difficult for other reasons. Celebrated in the major cities, the Stones found smaller audiences elsewhere. So their visits to Chess studios were partly designed by Oldham simply to raise the band's spirits. "The touring was to get a body of fans under our belts everywhere because we weren't selling any plastic. And these tours were not very successful that had gone before," said Oldham. "So they've been very good boys, 'I've got a present for you: we're going to go to Chess!' It's like telling the Pope you can go to the Vatican. It was very good for them, but it wasn't totally productive for my commercial aims. It tended to get a little too bluesy and go in a different type of streak than I was trying to encourage their songwriting."

Just three recordings from Chess would make it on to *Out Of Our Heads* – 'That's How Strong My Love Is', 'Have Mercy' and 'The Under Assistant West Coast Promotion Man'. The majority of the album was recorded at RCA, where the Stones found inspiration in the work of engineer Dave Hassinger, who was able to capture sounds and nuances that had so far eluded them. Not that many of these early sessions resulted in crisp and shiny tracks, not like the Beatles and their deluxe producer George Martin, whose records still sound clean enough to sit alongside the latest puddle of major-label syrup. True blues was still their aim. "We are recording in the US solely because we believe we can produce our best work there," Jagger said at the time.

Out Of Our Heads spent three weeks as America's top-selling album, but stalled at No. 2 in England. In retrospect, the British version of *Out Of Our Heads* was clearly inferior to the original US release, which included the songs 'Play With Fire' and '(Can't Get No) Satisfaction'. Because both tracks had already been released as singles, they were left off the record, robbing UK listeners of what otherwise would have been cornerstone tracks on *Out Of Our Heads*. "You did not put singles on albums," Oldham said of the Stones' UK releases. "Remember, we'd won the war but we

"WE WERE SUDDENLY GETTING THE REWARDS OF A TOTALLY INDEPENDENT LIFE. THIS WAS THE FIRST ALBUM WHERE WE WERE SEEING THE RESULTS OF BEING IN CONTROL OF OUR OWN LIVES."
ANDREW LOOG OLDHAM

29

had lost it. Not many people had that much money. So it was considered ripping people off."

The Stones were also busy in other ways. Charlie Watts published *Ode To A Flying Bird*, an illustrated children's book on the life of Charlie Parker he had written in 1961. Andrew Oldham released a ridiculous album via Decca called *The Rolling Stones Songbook* and credited to the Andrew Oldham Orchestra, with guest Keith Richards. The Stones' impresario also launched the Immediate record label, which would ultimately earn resentment from the band. And the Rolling Stones kept playing and recording, with little restriction.

GOTTA GET AWAY

This is Mick Jagger's idea of a love song, or a love-gone-wrong song, to be more precise. Either way, 'Gotta Get Away' gave an early taste of the Glimmer Twins' habit of exploring romance as an endlessly bitter confrontation. The indelicate treatment of women would emerge repeatedly in their work – 1978's *Some Girls* even saw Jagger listing varieties of women like items in a supermarket. There would be poignant exceptions to this theme, such as the deeply felt 'I Got The Blues', a heartbreaker from 1971 – we can blame the exit of Marianne Faithfull for that one. But 'Gotta Get Away' established a recurring motif for the Stones, where Jagger is never left in a relationship without the upper hand.

Indeed, 'Gotta Get Away' has the singer ending a love affair with some faceless chick in a tone of self-righteousness, when not drifting into cruel indifference – "To think I believed all your lies". Jagger is at once soothing and mocking in his phrasing, while the band builds a blithe folk-pop rhythm out of a blend of driving acoustic and electric guitars. The recently wed Charlie Watts keeps a steady beat, as he has done ever since through well over four decades of marriage. 'Gotta Get Away' is the first of many two-minute bursts of glib manhood.

HEART OF STONE

Recorded at RCA Studios in Hollywood, this lumbering anti-love ballad is part old blues and part Elvis-style torch song, except that Jagger denies any feeling whatsoever. Romance is a game he's won by shutting himself off from any sign of vulnerability. The message of 'Heart Of Stone' is almost numbing, as Jagger confesses "There've been so many girls that I've known, I've made so many cry". It's a puzzled revelation the singer mentions here with only passing interest. His concern isn't in understanding women, only in conquering them. The track did not appear in the US until 1966 as part of the *Big Hits (High Tide And Green Grass)* compilation. But even then, the Stones' statement on bad love didn't seem to scare off the little girls.

THE UNDER ASSISTANT WEST COAST PROMOTION MAN

The Rolling Stones were a very special case for London Records, the American arm of the Decca label. Jagger and his cohorts were clearly more than just another "British Invasion" act designed to cash in on a passing fad. The Stones had something else to offer. With roots firmly in the great blues tradition, their own sound and vision went deeper than 1960s pop. They were also Decca and London's last best hope of at least approaching the monumental success of the Beatles, who were then, as John Lennon would later famously quip, "bigger than Jesus" – at least to the young record-buying public. After all, Decca had passed on the Beatles, a decision that would later go down in A&R infamy. So now that the Stones were in their grasp, the label felt obliged to put their best men on the case.

In the US, that meant sending promotions man George Sherlock on the road with the Stones whenever they hit the West Coast. It actually got on the band's nerves at first – a chaperone was not what anyone had in mind, not with a full schedule of first-class debauchery ahead of them. And yet

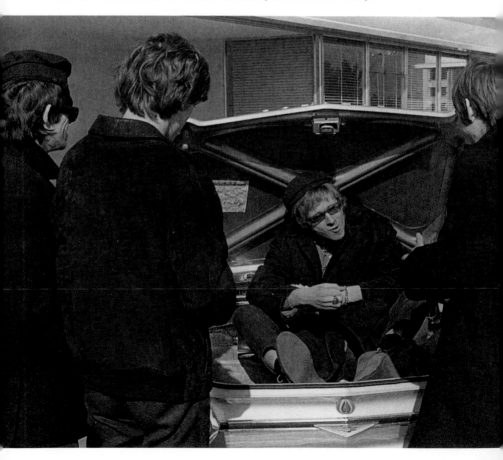

the presence of Mr Sherlock suggested that the label had actually made the Rolling Stones a top priority.

"There was a wonderful guy with a great wit called George Sherlock, who I think was *the* West Coast promotion man for London Records," Andrew Oldham recalled. "In England, promotion men never left their office, and we never saw a record. In America we saw both of these things, so we were slightly knocked out. To have a promotion man actually touring with you."

The band's reaction emerged via 'The Under Assistant West Coast Promotion Man', a biting satire on their experiences with poor Mr Sherlock. The last song to be credited to Nanker Phelge, the tune is an upbeat blues, with a twangy guitar melody mingling with heated harmonica lines. Jagger sings comically of a record company character with an inflated sense of importance – "Well, they laugh at my toupee, they sure put me down... I'm a necessary talent behind every rock and roll band".

'The Under Assistant West Coast Promotion Man' was first released in the US as the B-side to the 'Satisfaction' single. It was recorded at Chess in Chicago, with Oldham producing.

"Yeah, but he didn't know anything about blues," Jagger said of Oldham in 1968. "The cat who really got it together was Ron Malo, the engineer for Chess. He had been on all the original sessions."

I'M FREE

He really means it, man. It's as if Jagger and the boys had only just realized their unique place in society. By now it was clear that the Stones had somehow escaped the real-life limitations of working-class and middle-class Britain. They were now members of a new kind of royalty, where no whim was too ridiculous to be seriously considered. They were worshipped by young girls and Decca's accountants alike, celebrated in these innocent days before the drug raids, the divorces, the deaths and decay, and their eventual fate as rootless tax exiles.

IT WAS ANDREW LOOG OLDHAM *(CENTRE)* WHO HAD DEMANDED THAT JAGGER AND RICHARDS WRITE THEIR OWN MATERIAL.

For the time being, the band was happily able to weave a shimmering backdrop of blues-pop, while Jagger strutted to the very idea that he's "free to sing my song knowing it's out of trend". The singer further suggests that he's entitled to ANYTHING he wants, including the warmth and feminine comforts from the subject of his current affections. Not to celebrate, but to serve. It's all the same to him.

AFTERMATH

Recorded	December 1965 and March 1966, RCA Studios, Hollywood, California.
Produced by	Andrew Loog Oldham.
Musicians	The Rolling Stones: Mick Jagger (vocals, percussion, harmonica), Brian Jones (guitars, marimba, bells, Appalachian dulcimer, sitar, harpsichord, harmonica, keyboards, backing vocals), Keith Richards (guitar, backing vocals), Charlie Watts (drums, percussion, marimba, bells), Bill Wyman (bass guitar, marimba, bells, piano, organ, harpsichord). Additional musicians: Jack Nitzsche (percussion, piano, organ, harpsichord), Ian Stewart (piano, organ, harpsichord).

MOTHER'S LITTLE HELPER

STUPID GIRL

LADY JANE

UNDER MY THUMB

DONCHA BOTHER ME

GOIN' HOME

FLIGHT 505

HIGH AND DRY

OUT OF TIME

IT'S NOT EASY

I AM WAITING

TAKE IT OR LEAVE IT

THINK

WHAT TO DO

And now, re-introducing the Rolling Stones, new and improved for 1966. Or at any rate, different. These were no longer teenage blues copyists out to worship their black elders. The Stones were now making music entirely of their own creation. Anyone could have seen the changes coming. During the previous year, the band had enjoyed international chart-topping singles with 'Get Off Of My Cloud', '19th Nervous Breakdown' and 'Paint It Black', all of them mixing a strange new pop dementia with the band's blissful aggression. Here were the Stones basking in the elegance of pop without abandoning the primal code of the blues. Thus, the release of *Aftermath* would have seemed anticlimactic had it not been a cocksure manifesto of purpose for the Stones and an important milestone for the rock era.

HE MAY HAVE LOST CONTROL OVER OF HIS BAND, BUT BRIAN JONES CREATED A NEW ROLE FOR HIMSELF AS MULTI-INSTRUMENTALIST EXTRAORDINAIRE.

Aftermath was the first album written entirely by the suddenly thriving Jagger/Richards songwriting team. Not even Nanker Phelge was allowed to interfere with that monopoly – which of course meant that Jones, Watts and Wyman were now locked out of any publishing royalties. This was just as Andrew Loog Oldham had wanted, and of course he was right. Something new and dangerous was going on between the Glimmer Twins, who had discovered new ways to forge rich pop arrangements to their own dark ends. Tracks such as 'Mother's Little Helper' and 'Under My Thumb' were agitated tales, challenging an older generation while showing no mercy toward feminist notions of justice.

Brian Jones played no small part in this new development. Blues priest Elmo Lewis had become bored with his guitars, which were soon replaced in Brian's repertoire with a dazzling mix of sitar, dulcimer, marimbas and bells, as well as anything else picked up during his travels to the hills of North Africa. No instrument seemed too exotic or beyond his reach. Mick and Keith were quickly taking over the band he'd first imagined as a boy back in Cheltenham, but Jones remained a powerful musical force within the Rolling Stones.

These were developments that their friends back at Chess might have had trouble understanding. And yet the Stones were making an important statement with *Aftermath*, demonstrating to the pop masses and the blues purists alike that the blues were simply a beginning for them – a step on the road to creating a sound for their own age. They would ultimately return to the songs of Chicago and the Mississippi Delta in coming years, but then it would be by choice, not necessity.

The Rolling Stones were hardly the only band of young British blues purists to edge ever deeper into rock and pop. Just as the Yardbirds, the Animals, Them and others experimented in newer styles – even if they sometimes earned the wrath of hardcore fans – the Stones found themselves inevitably drawn to the exciting new musical possibilities in the air.

"I found it logical," says London blues devotee John Mayall, who has led his Bluesbreakers through three decades of blues devotion. "Everybody was very young and drawn to the electrification of the guitars and the music of Bo Diddley, Chuck Berry and Muddy Waters. That was a starting point really for them as musicians. They had to find their own way of expression. That kind of led them into the areas that just happened to make them very popular on the rock and roll pop scene. In all cases, everyone ended up finding their own identity. The blues was their starting point."

The sounds of *Aftermath* emerged during two intense periods of work at RCA Studios in Hollywood: five days in December 1965, followed by two weeks the following March. Visitors from Phil Spector to Brian Wilson of the Beach Boys often stopped by, usually just to observe, but sometimes to participate.

The Stones were deep into their own creative revolution, but not everyone was happy with their share of the credit. "There was injustice in the way some songs came to be written and credited solely to Mick and Keith," Wyman noted in his autobiography. "Experimenting in the studio, Brian or I often contributed a riff or a suggestion that was adopted and became a vital part of the song."

By the time *Aftermath* made its April debut in the UK (and June in the US) the entire band could bask in the afterglow of yet another No. 1 album, just as they embarked on a fifth American tour. So what if the unbeatable Beatles remained masters of the widest spectrum of pop culture? The Rolling Stones had their own music to make. They had their own destiny to chase.

"That was a big landmark record for me," Jagger told *Rolling Stone* magazine in 1995. "It was the first time we wrote the whole record and finally laid to rest the ghost of having to do these very nice and interesting, no doubt, but still cover versions of old R&B songs – which we really didn't feel we were doing justice, to be perfectly honest, particularly because we didn't have the maturity."

MOTHER'S LITTLE HELPER

What a drag it is getting old". Mick's not kidding. And this was no accidental affront to his elders, but a jeering statement for a new generation whose time was fast approaching.

All of this undoubtedly came as alarming news to the Dean Martin generation, who had won the war and built the suburban dream for every middle-class family from Burbank to Bristol. Now the Rolling Stones were talking about things that were best left unsaid. 'Mother's Little Helper' is the diary of a mad housewife, designed to discredit that post-war, pre-fab existence while exposing a deep sadness just beneath the surface.

Jagger sings about a housewife who resorts to some mysterious pep pills (amphetamines? valium?) to get her through her days of instant cake and frozen dinners, serving an inattentive husband, whose presence is barely felt in her world. "The pursuit of happiness just seems a bore," Mick goes on, and mother's dose gets heavier with every passing day.

Dissatisfaction with society as it is, and the mundane life it encourages, is a recurring theme in the Jagger/Richards songbook – examine, for example, 'Have You Seen Your Mother, Baby, Standing in the Shadow?'. "Mick's always written a lot about it," Richards told *Rolling Stone* in 1971. "A lot of the stuff Chuck Berry and early rock writers did was putting down that other generation. We used to laugh at those people but they must have gotten the message right away because they tried to put rock and roll down, trying to get it off the radio, off records. Obviously they saw some destruction stemming from it… they felt it right away."

As recorded, the song is a muddy tangle of acoustic guitars, given jarring definition from a twangy sitar riff played by Brian Jones. The primitive sitar experiments of Jones and George Harrison initially alarmed the likes of master Ravi Shankar, but without them mid-sixties pop music would not have been the same. The songwriting duties were fairly evenly divided between the Glimmer Twins. In most cases, Mick handled the writing of the words and Keith the music, although Richards would often come up with a single lyric or phrase that would act as a title or chorus. Most of the writing was also done on the road, and recorded between concert gigs. "An American tour meant you started writing another album," said Richards. "After three, four weeks, you had enough and then you went to LA and recorded it. We worked very fast that way and when you came off a tour you were shit hot playing, as hot as the band is gonna be."

"EVERYONE ENDED UP FINDING THEIR OWN IDENTITY. THE BLUES WAS THEIR STARTING POINT."

JOHN MAYALL

37

STUPID GIRL

The increasing anti-female tenor of the Stones repertoire should have been a warning to Chrissie Shrimpton, Mick's long-suffering girlfriend. If women were frequently the obsessive subject of Jagger/Richards compositions, they were also depicted as being untrustworthy and disposable.

'Stupid Girl'? Just who was Mick talking about? Poor Chrissie may have got her answer the following year, when she attempted suicide after Jagger abruptly abandoned her for singer Marianne Faithfull. Of course, there was no shortage of female companionship in the world of the Rolling Stones. Young women wept at their very presence. Previously unapproachable royals and debutantes lined up to meet young Mick. He certainly obliged, but with an increasingly critical eye.

On 'Stupid Girl', Jagger turns bitter as he cruelly picks apart the deceptive facade he's perceived on the women he's met. Not even the finest makeup, shoes, hair and comely good looks can disguise their dubious intentions. "She's the worst thing in this world!" Jagger shouts across a bed of organ sounds and a flash of light guitar duelling at the bridge.

"Obviously, I was having a bit of trouble," Jagger explained in 1995. "I wasn't in a good relationship. Or I was in too many bad relationships. I had so many girlfriends at that point. None of them seemed to care they weren't pleasing me very much. I was obviously in with the wrong group."

LADY JANE

The true measure of any great mid-sixties pop band was an ability to shift gears, to move convincingly from one musical extreme to the next. Both the Beatles and Kinks drifted effortlessly from tough-guy rock to achingly sweet balladry. Now that the Rolling Stones were deep into their own pop period, they could do no less. So even if it was ludicrous to set the anti-chick diatribes of 'Under My Thumb' and 'Stupid Girl' around the suddenly romantic 'Lady Jane', the Stones pulled it off from the sheer force of their shared personality.

The band had already demonstrated a knack for this sort of thing just the previous December with 'As Tears Go By', originally written for Marianne Faithfull, and a top-10 hit in America for the Stones. Light pop balladry may have had nothing to do with the roaring gutbucket rock and blues that would constitute the band's greatest legacy, but it was a necessity for the mid-sixties Stones. ('Lady Jane' was, in fact, omitted from the US release of *Aftermath*, and would not appear until the US-only *Flowers* compilation.)

'Lady Jane' opens with Keith Richards picking quietly at an acoustic guitar and Brian Jones elegantly tapping at a dulcimer. They're joined by Jack Nitzsche on harpsichord as a strangely devotional Mick Jagger recites a love letter, declaring himself "your humble servant".

Chrissie Shrimpton assumed the song was for her, though early press accounts suggested it was based on the story of King Henry VIII and Jane Seymour, his third wife. Seymour was one of Henry's few wives to be spared the executioner's blade, although she died from complications of childbirth after bearing the king's only song, Edward, in 1537.

"I don't really know what that's all about, myself," Mick said in 1968. "All the names are historical but it was really unconscious that they should fit together from the same period." In 1971, Keith told *Rolling Stone*, "Brian was getting into dulcimer then… We were also listening to a lot of Appalachian music then, too. To me, 'Lady Jane' is very Elizabethan. There are a few places in England where people still speak that way, Chaucer English."

UNDER MY THUMB

More good vibes from the chivalrous Mick Jagger. The songwriting of the Glimmer Twins had now progressed beyond the struggle to simply craft a commercial pop nugget. Rolling Stones songs now reflected the ideas and attitudes of the songwriters themselves. But what were they saying? The singer has said the driving rock assault of 'Under My Thumb' was simply a distasteful reply to one particularly unpleasant woman. Just a caricature, he insisted, not an anti-feminist diatribe – "It's a bit of a jokey number, really."

Whatever the inspiration may have been, 'Under My Thumb' was a powerful track, with Jagger emerging as a hypnotically self-righteous frontman. He sings in a rough, jeering tone, bragging about his power over a young woman who once dominated him. Now Jagger has her in a pathetically submissive role, even deciding for her what clothes she is to wear – "She's the sweetest pet in the world, she does just what she's told". His repetition of the song's title says it all.

Equally effective on the song is the spirited tapping of marimbas by Brian Jones, leading the Stones into some new musical territory. Yet the dark textures Jones and the band were extracting from otherwise pleasant pop owed something to the grim blues hoodoo of their recent past. "That riff played on marimbas really makes it," Jagger said in 1995. "Plus the groove it gets in the end of the tune. It speeds up, actually. And it becomes this kind of groove tune at the end... and then it became a thing feminists fastened on."

The song took on a whole new meaning at the end of 1969, when it served as a horrific soundtrack to the murder of Meredith Hunter at Altamont. A song about the struggle between men and women, and between the classes, was now transformed into something darker than even Jagger had intended.

DONCHA BOTHER ME

"AN AMERICAN TOUR MEANT THAT YOU STARTED WRITING ANOTHER ALBUM. AFTER THREE, FOUR WEEKS YOU HAD ENOUGH AND THEN YOU WENT TO LA AND RECORDED IT."
KEITH RICHARDS

Brian Jones creates a reasonable facsimile of the Mississippi Delta blues on this track with fiery bottleneck guitar, set against Keith's sharp riffing and a thumping heartbeat from Charlie Watts. It wasn't going to get them on the pop charts, but the Stones were still happy to drift back into a heavy blues mode.

'Doncha Bother Me' is a convincing version of the blues, and a precursor to the edgy decadence that would later emerge on *Exile On Main Street*. Not that the sentiment here cuts a great deal deeper than the song's self-explanatory title. In 1966, Jagger's message was a simple rant, perhaps directed at the growing crowd of hangers-on surrounding the Stones.

GOIN' HOME

At just over 11 minutes, 'Goin' Home' was *Aftermath*'s strangest exercise. It was more a loose jam session than a finished song, and was at once an earthy throwback to the Stones' early blues days and a shimmering glimpse of the coming psychedelic era. The track's length and aimlessness also shattered any limits of sense, going well beyond the usual three-minute boundary. Still, 'Goin' Home' was finally more successful conceptually than as a worthwhile musical experience.

Singing across understated layers of harmonica, guitar and piano, Jagger huffs and puffs with conviction. He hadn't yet mastered the vocal improvisation that would become second nature by the 1970s, so he claps his hands to the bluesy, trance-like rhythm, repeating, "Well, come on! Come on!" What else was there to do?

"It was the first long rock and roll cut," Keith Richards said in 1971. "It broke that two-minute barrier. We tried to make singles as long as we could do them because we like to just let things roll on. No one sat down to make an 11 minute track. The song was written just the first two and a half minutes. We just happened to keep the tape rolling."

'Goin' Home' sounded much like the early Stones, if not for the echoing, almost psychedelic vibe at the edges. The track's all-night session was hosted by Andrew Oldham at RCA Studios in Hollywood. Brian Wilson was one visitor, along with the dancers Terri Garr (later a successful actress) and Toni Basil (later a choreographer and singer) from TV's *Shindig*. LA scene-maker Rodney Bingenheimer, once dubbed the mayor of the Sunset Strip, remembers seeing a white duck wandering the studio. There was also a young African American groupie wearing a long fur coat and, apparently, nothing else. Outside was a crowd of kids, all hoping desperately for a glimpse of some rock star, preferably one of the Stones.

Inside, Jagger sang 'Goin' Home' over and over again. "Mick Jagger had a hand-held mike and was on his knees, singing 'Goin' home, I'm goin' home'," says Bingenheimer, who remembers Mick as wearing a striped button-up shirt, and Keith in a leather coat and shades. "It was really long. The whole night was like one song."

Bingenheimer came across Jagger again that year at Phil Spector's session for Ike and Tina Turner's epic 'River Deep Mountain High' at Hollywood's Gold Star Studios. Brian Wilson was also visiting. And Bingenheimer noticed some similarities between the sessions. "They worshipped Phil Spector," says Bingenheimer, who later worked as a local club owner and a radio personality. "And whenever Phil Spector produces a record, he has an audience. He puts on a show. Maybe Mick got that idea."

FLIGHT 505

Recording in LA, touring Australia, wives and girlfriends back in Britain, Ed Sullivan in New York, Christmas with the folks at home… The Rolling Stones spent much of their youth in the air, crossing the Atlantic with the frequency of a cross-town commuter. How strange then that Jagger and the band could so happily describe the crashing of a passenger plane into the sea on 'Flight 505'.

Mick's morbid streak had the singer imagining a fate similar that of the Buddy Holly, Ritchie Valens and the Big Bopper, all killed when their small plane crashed into Clear Lake on February 3, 1959. Jagger sings to some glancing Chuck Berry-style chords and boogie-woogie piano, doubtless played by Ian Stewart. The band's later membership of the so-called "jet-set" suggests that if Jagger had any lingering fears of flying, they were quickly overcome.

CHRIS FARLOWE *(RIGHT)* TOPPED THE UK POP CHARTS WITH HIS VERSION OF 'OUT OF TIME'.

HIGH AND DRY

Here is an early blast of folk rock masquerading as country. Despite some spirited harmonica, 'High And Dry' comes closer to a kind of hillbilly skiffle sound, not unlike some of the Beatles' acoustic tracks of the period.

Accompanied by Bill Wyman's thumping bass lines and the crashing cymbals of Charlie Watts, Jagger sings of being dropped by a rich girl without much regret. At first glance, 'High And Dry' seems to depict the girl as being in control, far from a prisoner under Jagger's thumb. And yet the song's situation was almost certainly inspired by Jagger's own life as a Rolling Stone, where some women were certainly attracted less to young Michael Philip Jagger than to his fabulous fame and fortune.

OUT OF TIME

Although Brian again plays the marimbas to amusing effect, it's overwhelmingly Mick's performance – both intimate and seeped in attitude – that carries the moving 'Out Of Time' The sound is pure Motown pop, with a casually sensuous Jagger snapping his fingers with utter self-confidence and pity, much like a punk prowling the streets of West Side Story and ignoring the girl at his heels.

"You're out of touch, my baby, my poor discarded baby," Jagger sings with an air of superiority as he tells of brushing off a girlfriend who had once abandoned him, much to her later regret. He's moved on, but even if he hadn't, this moment of revenge would be too sweet to let go. She must suffer as he did.

Though too often lost in the crowd of mid-sixties Jagger/Richards songs, 'Out Of Time' landed the Stones within their own cruel brand of soul music. There's nothing here to remind listeners of their unfortunate attempts at 'Under The Boardwalk' and 'My Girl'. And not even the few seconds of flat, nasal Bill Wyman singing backup can destroy the moment. Although Chris Farlowe's more compassionate reading the following year would hit No. 1 on the British singles chart, Jagger's typically self-absorbed performance is definitive.

'Out Of Time' was another song left off the American release of *Aftermath*, emerging later on the *Flowers* compilation.

IT'S NOT EASY

While *Aftermath* was an important step for the Stones, the album's second half inevitably lacked the impact of those first tracks. What could compete with the energy and social impact of 'Mother's Little Helper'? Indeed, most of these later songs would rarely emerge again even as part of the band's live playlist. This is not to say that *Aftermath*'s final tracks are mere fillers, except in the context of their coming accomplishments. With its driving rhythm, Chuck Berry riffing, and Mick's moaning chorus about being abandoned by his woman, a song like 'It's Not Easy' holds up well in most other company. If his expression of loneliness is not entirely convincing, Jagger at least treats the female character in the song with affection and regret.

I AM WAITING

It's a long journey from Elmore James to the innocence of 'I Am Waiting', but the Rolling Stones find the right mood here via folky acoustic guitars and Brian Jones' dulcimer. This is the young Stones at their most convincingly romantic, making pop that explodes into moments of yearning.

Jagger's lyrics are unusually obscure, erupting during the chorus to fine melodramatic effect – a method Bill Wyman would put to use for his 'In Another Land' on *Their Satanic Majesties Request*. Mick sings in embracing, soothing tones, and shows rare restraint during the quieter moments, followed with bursts of emotion.

TAKE IT OR LEAVE IT

'Take It Or Leave It' sounds like any number of the early, easily forgotten Jagger/Richards originals written under orders from Andrew Oldham.

As recorded, it is a shapeless misfire, a flat gathering of acoustic chords, accented with the delicate ring of finger cymbals. Although the song is performed with conviction, it leads nowhere. Aftermath would have been a better album without it, a fact that must have occurred to London Records, who omitted the song from the album's US release – it would not emerge until the *Flowers* compilation came out in 1967.

Just why the Searchers would choose to cover this particular Jagger/ Richards composition is one of pop music's great mysteries.

THINK

'Think' begins promisingly enough, propelled by an uptempo, fuzzy rock sound. Charlie Watts keeps a steady, driving beat as the rest of the Stones build a formidable wall of sound, with baritone guitar chords that succeed in filling the air like a full horn section. And yet it's a song that never fully takes off, even with Jagger's hectoring lecture at some girl to look back at her mistakes – "Tell me whose fault was that, babe?" he sings to her. The vocal melody only rarely strays far from a basic, flat reading.

Chris Farlowe had already released his own ignored version of 'Think' on Andrew Oldham's Immediate Records in January 1966. The Stones version was equally unsuccessful in reaching the pop masses.

45

WHAT TO DO

'What To Do' was an odd place to conclude an album which otherwise represented significant growth for the Rolling Stones. This paean to boredom had little or nothing to do with where the Stones had been, and even less to do with where their sound was going. There were no blues here. No rock and roll. Just a simple mixture of acoustic and electric guitar that sounded closer to early Mersey Beat, with the bizarre addition of "bow-bow-bow!" backing vocals that could easily have been stolen from the Beach Boys.

This was the age of experimentation. If the content of *Aftermath* and the fast approaching *Between The Buttons* indicated a commitment to smoother pop ideas, it was really only a passing phase. Songs such as 'Out Of Time' and 'Under My Thumb' displayed the Stones new mastery of the genre, but it was evidently not where their ultimate commitment lay. Producer and manager Andrew Loog Oldham certainly encouraged the Stones toward the most lucrative commercial sound available, but Keith Richards was a rock player to the core, and he was only then emerging as a dominant force in the band. None of the Stones could know that their most serious work was yet to come, in an era defined by their definition of rock and roll.

BETWEEN THE BUTTONS

Recorded	August to December 1966, RCA Studios, Hollywood, California; Olympic Studios, London.
Produced by	Andrew Loog Oldham.
Musicians	Mick Jagger (vocals, percussion), Brian Jones (organ, vibraphone, accordion, harmonica, recorder, percussion, kazoo, saxophone, dulcimer, marimba, theremin, harpsichord, guitar , piano, sitar, trumpet, horn, trombone, backing vocals), Keith Richards (guitar, backing vocals, bass guitar, piano, organ, double bass), Charlie Watts (drums, percussion), Bill Wyman (bass guitar, percussion, double bass, backing vocals). Additional musicians: Jack Nitzsche (piano, harpsichord, percussion, horn arrangements), Ian Stewart (piano and organ).

YESTERDAY'S PAPERS
MY OBSESSION
BACK STREET GIRL
CONNECTION
SHE SMILED SWEETLY
COOL, CALM AND COLLECTED
ALL SOLD OUT
PLEASE GO HOME
WHO'S BEEN SLEEPING HERE?
COMPLICATED
MISS AMANDA JONES
SOMETHING HAPPENED TO ME YESTERDAY

SOME GIRLS? THE ROLLING STONES CROSS THE GREAT SEXUAL DIVIDE.

Don't even mention *Between The Buttons* to Mick Jagger. For him, it's an album best left forgotten, a failed experiment at multi-layered pop. That's a sour verdict for what is still among the most beloved albums of the band's mid-sixties pop phase. Frank Zappa always spoke highly of it. So have critics and members of rock bands as diverse as the Doors and Fleetwood Mac. But Mick will have none of it. *Between The Buttons* is forever spoiled for him by the four-track recording process, which saw layer after layer of fancy overdubs muddle the pristine pop sound he'd once imagined for it. Jagger was still complaining about it two decades later.

"Oh, I hate that fucking record," the singer moaned to engineer Dave Jerden during the making of *Dirty Work* in 1986. To Jagger, *Between The Buttons* was just one more good reason for the Rolling Stones to finally abandon the ways of pure pop in favour of their coming blend of rock and blues – even if that didn't actually occur until after the half-baked psychedelia of 1967's *Their Satanic Majesties Request*. The sounds of Chicago and the Mississippi Delta were beckoning Jagger and the Stones once again.

Of course, the band was enjoying the fruits of pop stardom just the same, hanging out with the young Guinness heir Tara Brown in Ireland, spending Christmas in Los Angeles, moving into slick new pads in the UK – Keith into a thatched Tudor mansion named *Redlands*, Mick into an apartment at the heart of fashionable London. The *Aftermath* album had been another success, as were the singles of 'Paint It Black' and 'Have You Seen Your Mother, Baby, Standing In The Shadow?'. Even Chris Farlowe's version of 'Out Of Time', produced by the Glimmer Twins themselves, hit No. 1 in England. Stones tours of the UK and North America were met with the usual hysteria: rioting in Montreal, London fans knocking down Keith and nearly strangling Mick after rushing the stage at the Royal Albert Hall.

"We were in danger of becoming respectable," Richards happily said at the time. "But now the new wave has arrived, rushing the stage just like old times."

In the midst of their American tour, the Stones stopped in Hollywood for nine days of recording at RCA Studios, where they began the sessions for what would become *Between The Buttons*. But the bulk of the album would be recorded at Olympic Studios in London. When it was finished, *Between The Buttons* was further away from the band's core blues sources than any Stones album so far. At this time, the Stones were making waves of pure pop, and the results were frequently brilliant, in spite of Jagger's later disappointment.

The American version of the album deleted 'Back Street Girl' and 'Please Go Home' in favour of 'Ruby Tuesday' and 'Let's Spend The Night Together', which had already been released as singles in the UK. *Between The Buttons* was the final Stones album to have a different song list on opposite sides of the Atlantic, suggesting that the band was assuming more control over their music and career. It was the inevitable result of the success the Stones had enjoyed almost from the beginning. Unlike much of their earlier work, *Between The Buttons* was not recorded quickly between gigs in the US. Instead, the Stones camped out at Olympic Studios in London, ready to follow their muse where it took them.

In his 1990 autobiography, *Stone Alone*, Bill Wyman calls the album the "first studio session at which we concentrated on an album as a finished product."

"Working with the Rolling Stones never really changed," engineer Glyn Johns told journalist Craig Rosen in 1994. "Immediately they became successful enough to not have any financial restrictions on their recording budget. They did take an immense amount of time making a record. And they very rarely did any preparation before going in the studio. Most of the material throughout the period that I worked with them they wrote in the studio. They would play stuff for extremely long periods of time before they ever got a take that they were satisfied with. I found that extremely monotonous."

Those habits would ultimately drive away Johns, who liked to work quickly and found that he could complete three or four albums with other bands in the same amount of time. Johns had been the first man to record the Stones, even before their discovery by Andrew Oldham, and he engineered most of their important albums throughout the sixties. He reunited briefly with the band during the making of 1976's *Black And Blue*, before moving on to work as a producer of bands ranging from the Eagles to the Clash. But his legacy with the Rolling Stones has haunted his reputation ever since. "It was fascinating working with them because of the abilities and personalities," Johns said. "A lot of the music they made I thought was amazing. I just didn't particularly appreciate the way they went about doing it... So in the end I quit. I wanted to produce, and I wanted to be recognized as a producer, which I never was going to be by the Rolling Stones. And I wanted to do something other than sit and wait for someone to show up, which is what I spent a large portion of my youth doing.

"I am really proud to have been involved with the records I made with them. Although when anybody asks me about working with them my memories are not tremendously pleasant – there was a lot of boredom involved – the fact is that when they played and got it together it was fantastic. They were unbeatable and I'm really glad that I was around. I don't regret a minute I spent with them. I think we made some fucking great records."

For many listeners, one of the greatest of those records remains *Between The Buttons*. It was the Stones' richest pop moment, but beneath the surface things were beginning to fray at the margins. Drugs had gradually entered the scene, and soon had a devastating impact on the musical contribution of Brian Jones.

For the album cover session with photographer Gered Mankowitz, the band was somehow gathered at dawn. The resulting photograph was made with Vaseline smeared across the camera lens, and captures the Stones at their most bleary eyed and dishevelled. Only Keith looks utterly composed – probably because he had not bothered to sleep the night before. The picture's blurred edges suggest a fragmenting, psychedelic vibe. And at the center of the image is Jones, a spaced-out grin across his lips, his eyes swollen and unfocused, sinking obliviously into his coat. It was a telling image. Jones was still a key creative player within the Stones, but the golden-haired multi-instrumentalist was already beginning to lose touch with the world.

"OH, I HATE THAT FUCKING RECORD!" MICK JAGGER DELIVERS HIS VERDICT ON THE NEW ALBUM

49

YESTERDAY'S PAPERS

'Yesterday's Papers' is the first song Mick Jagger ever wrote on his own for a Rolling Stones album, but its ambivalent tone and suggestion that girlfriends are as disposable as yesterday's newspaper was hardly a new theme from these masters of misogyny. The song was likely inspired by Jagger's just-ended relationship with live-in girlfriend Chrissie Shrimpton. She had survived a recent car crash with her famous boyfriend, but now could only watch in horror as young Mick made his first public appearance with a singer named Marianne Faithfull at the launch party for the *International Times* underground newspaper. For Jagger, women were easily replaced.

"Who wants yesterday's girl?" asks Jagger at the song's opening, singing with a typically cruel detachment. His very public life has been one of "constant change", he explains, and now a change is long overdue in his sex life. The song is a two-minute farewell to Miss Shrimpton, a "horrible public humiliation" for poor Chrissie, according to Faithfull. They were unofficially engaged when Jagger broke up with his once-fashionable girlfriend of three years in December 1966.

"We were very much in love but we argued all the time," Shrimpton bravely explained at the time. "As time goes on you begin to feel different about life and each other. There wasn't a row. We broke by mutual agreement." Soon enough, Shrimpton attempted suicide, with Jagger refusing to pay her hospital bill. Instead, he had all her belongings removed from his home.

The lyrics of 'Yesterday's Papers' may have been about Mick's indifference to heartbreak and abandonment, but the music behind him was completely upbeat and hypnotic. It was a festive blend of marimbas, harpsichord, unidentified wind instruments, the low, low rumble of bass, brief shards of guitar and overlapping vocals, straddling the right and left stereo channels. The final mix offered a more natural psychedelic excursion than much of the coming *Their Satanic Majesties Request*.

The richness of instrumentation on 'Yesterday's Papers' and elsewhere across *Between The Buttons* owed much to Brian Jones, who had created a new role for himself within the band by *Aftermath*. His ability to wrestle interesting new sounds from whatever exotic instruments were within his reach put an indelible stamp on the Stones' pop era. His later firing from the band shortly before his death in 1969 inevitably stripped the Stones

"I THINK THERE MUST BE SOME TANGIBLE ELEMENT THAT HE WAS BRINGING TO THE GROUP, YOU KNOW, THAT KEPT IT FROM BEING TOO 'CHUCK BERRY'." FLEETWOOD MAC'S LINDSEY BUCKINGHAM ON BRIAN JONES

back down to a straight-ahead rock and roll band. As glorious as the post-Jones era would be, there was a certain charm and excitement about the Stones' mid-sixties pop records, which remain as deeply influential on later acts as anything else in the Jagger/Richards catalogue.

For singer-guitarist Lindsey Buckingham, whose version of Fleetwood Mac found international success in the mid-seventies, often by exploring his band's own troubled relationships, the Brian Jones-era Rolling Stones was deeply influential. His favourite Stones albums are those with a sense of "the European and the element of colour and the ability to try things that Brian Jones brought in. I think there must be some intangible element that he was bringing to the group, you know, that kept it from being too 'Chuck Berry'. There's some brilliant things on *Between The Buttons*. That was a good run they had there."

MY OBSESSION

This is what Mick was complaining about: the muddled wall of sound, Ian Stewart's piano banging hopelessly in the distance, leaving only the vocals with any clarity. Blame producer-manager Andrew Loog Oldham. "Andrew used to think that anything was possible if you put enough echo on it," Richards said later.

It's just not the kind of thing Jagger had in mind when he sketched out these nonsensical lyrics, with his scattered ideas about girls who need *teaching*, and built mostly around words that rhyme with "obsession". But the fans ate it up, taking *Between The Buttons* into the top three on both sides of the Atlantic. That's not quite as successful as other Stones records of the period, but reasonably popular just the same. Jagger would rather just forget about these tracks. "I don't think I thought they were very good at the time either," he said.

BACK STREET GIRL

'Back Street Girl' was an early sign of the Rolling Stones' interest in the country/folk-flavoured pop that would re-emerge with great effect on *Beggar's Banquet*. The song enjoys a delicate mixture of acoustic picking, light percussion and swells of accordion. It's a sound that suggests warmth and affection. And yet Jagger's vocals are typically casual and cruel, singing

to some poor "back street girl", and instructing her to service him sexually at his pleasure. Just don't bother his wife or call him at home.

Is 'Back Street Girl' wry social commentary on the downtrodden classes, or condescending male fantasy gone crazy? Whatever you may think, it's an affecting package, and the only song on *Between The Buttons* that Jagger remembers with any fondness.

In a pop era dominated by the Beatles, the songcraft of the Rolling Stones was too often overlooked, argues Mick Fleetwood, the drummer with Fleetwood Mac. His own band had emerged from the same London blues scene that launched the Stones. Both the Beatles and Stones remain his favourite bands of all time. "The Stones really put some vibrant stuff together," says Fleetwood, also a veteran of John Mayall's Bluesbreakers. "They wrote great songs, and they still do. The image of the Stones sometimes denigrated their worth as creative people."

CONNECTION

Keith Richards is a rocker, a committed denizen of the road, devoted to bringing rock and roll to stages across the continents, but even he sometimes longs for home. 'Connection' addresses that yearning, and describes a life spent in airports, making and missing connections. It's a life of endless inoculations from worried doctors, and of irritating searches of his bags by customs officials seeking contraband. Illicit drugs would not enter the Stones story for a few more months, when the band was busted at *Redlands*, Keith's country home. For now, it was a futile search. "They're dying to add me to their collection," sings a slightly frantic Jagger.

'Connection' is a hard, pop nugget, composed more or less by Richards alone. The guitarist fires off a series of rough, Chuck Berry chords, mingling with an effective minimalist piano melody. Richards' voice harmonizes roughly with Jagger's, and Charlie Watts slaps a fierce, steady beat. Even then, simplicity was Keith's calling card, at a time when Eric Clapton and other new blues heroes were taking rock guitar to new extremes. The Stones were equally versed in the blues, but their interpretations were somehow different.

"They were always about songs, and they weren't about long fucking guitar solos," says Mick Farren, a member of the Deviants in the mid-sixties and a writer for the *International Times*. "They were really pushing the envelope, beginning with 'Satisfaction'. What the Stones were doing retained a massive amount of R&B power."

A commitment to simplicity would remain a key element of the Stones' music for decades. "I don't think rock and roll songwriters should worry about art," Keith Richards said in 1986. "I don't think it comes into it. A lot of it is just craft anyway, especially after doing it for a long time. As far as I'm concerned, art is just short for Arthur."

SHE SMILED SWEETLY

Young Mick Jagger is actually in awe of a woman on 'She Smiled Sweetly'. Ignore, if you can, all of those earlier messages of misogynistic hate and despair, Jagger's endless battle of the sexes, and drift into his arms. Mick is capable of love after all. Maybe not romantic love, but at least a weakness for warm, maternal guidance, and a source of wisdom to soothe his battered soul.

His voice erupts from ripples of solemn organ melodies, piano and the thick basslines of Bill Wyman. Master troubadour Bob Dylan is a perceptible influence on both the lyrics and Jagger's soothing delivery. It's all comfort and happiness, an unexpectedly humane sentiment from Britain's most notorious rock and roll hoodlums.

Not unprecedented, heartfelt balladry has been a recurring motif in the Rolling Stones legacy, from 'As Tears Go By' to 'Angie' in the early 1970s. "I always loved that Mick could write something as sensitive as 'As Tears Goes By'," says Fleetwood Mac's Lindsey Buckingham. "It always blew my mind that he had that streak in him, underneath all that other stuff."

53

COOL, CALM AND COLLECTED

According to Andy Johns, "Nicky Hopkins was the best fucking rock and roll pianist who ever lived, apart from Jerry Lee Lewis." That's heavy praise, but Johns had ample opportunity to watch the man at work, first as visiting little brother to engineer Glyn Johns, and then while working himself as engineer on Stones albums stretching from *Sticky Fingers* to *It's Only Rock 'N' Roll*. Hopkins is a central figure on *Between The Buttons*, sending piano flourishes across tracks of various styles and moods. On 'Cool, Calm And Collected', he plays a vague approximation of ragtime as Mick Jagger adopts the tone of a Vaudevillian carnival barker, singing of a girl who is far too together, too competent, too independent, too wealthy, too respected, for his comfort. At the chorus, Brian Jones strums a sitar and Jagger's voice suddenly floats into the ether, as he adopts a mocking tone toward the supercool chick beyond his reach: "She knows all the right games to play."

The song is dark and comical, concluding with an accelerating thrash of drums, guitar, kazoo and harmonica. It's a lighthearted finish, much as the Stones would repeat later via 'On With The Show' at the close of 1967's *Their Satanic Majesties Request*.

ALL SOLD OUT

Anger becomes the Stones. There's a convincing, raw quality to Mick Jagger's vocals on 'All Sold Out'. The song curdles in his throat, and is matched with some tense guitar work from Keith Richards, whose playing here is exceptionally reckless and dangerous. The guitars burst free from the sonic muddle of *Between The Buttons*. And Wyman and Watts thunder behind the Glimmer Twins, as Brian Jones blows on flute quietly within the blistering rock mix. Jagger is outraged at some unmentioned betrayal. The intensity of the performance suggests the anger is real.

PLEASE GO HOME

The shimmering beat behind Mick Jagger on 'Please Go Home' – which owes much to Bo Diddley – was just the starting point for the Rolling Stones on this strange psychedelic experiment. Charlie Watts smashes at the cymbals with extra fervour as Andrew Loog Oldham and the band overlay a dizzying array of echo effects and extra-sloppy guitars. Once again, the song appeared only on the UK version of *Between The Buttons*, and was not released in America until it appeared on the *Flowers* compilation released six months later. Bo Diddley would certainly have recognized his trademark rhythm, but very little else.

WHO'S BEEN SLEEPING HERE?

Clapton wasn't God. Not while the likes of Jimi Hendrix still inhabited the earth. Guitar heroes were easy to come by in 1967. Less common was the kind of genre-shattering voice epitomized by Bob Dylan. Decades before he was entombed in legend, Saint Bob was merely the most dynamic songwriter of his generation, and a monumental influence on his contemporaries, from the Beatles and the Byrds to Hendrix and the Rolling Stones.

NOT EVEN THE BEATLES OR STONES COULD ESCAPE THE MONUMENTAL INFLUENCE OF BOB DYLAN.

55

Dylan – born Robert Zimmerman – emerged from Duluth, Minnesota, as an edgy folk troubadour, drawing on the work of Woody Guthrie and the "Beat" writers, such as Kerouac, Ginsberg and Burroughs. After making

a pilgrimage to Guthrie's deathbed, Dylan landed in Manhattan's Greenwich Village, where audiences discovered his explosive protest anthems and reflective folk, which often reached for a poetry utterly devoid of pretension. His songs were instead drenched in attitude, straight talk, mythic characters and ironic wordplay that was as devastating as it was amusing. By the time he "went electric" and embraced rock and roll in 1965, Dylan was the indisputable poet laureate of pop.

"Bob showed us all in the sixties a new approach, new ways of writing songs," Richards said in 1992. "He came from a folk tradition, which had much looser possibilities, and he showed you that rock and roll didn't have to be quite so restricted by that verse-chorus-verse formula."

Dylan was cocky, too. He once told Richards that he could have written '(Can't Get No) Satisfaction', but that the Stones could not have written his 'Desolation Row'. But Jagger later responded: "I'd like to hear Dylan *sing* 'Satisfaction'."

And Dylan's influence can be heard loud and clear within the organic grooves of 'Who's Been Sleeping Here'. Jagger sings to a lover, demanding to know who's been sleeping in his bed, and eating off his plate, in his absence. The singer's imagery is plainly Dylanesque, and so is the music: the folky acoustic guitars and harmonica, the steady piano melody. Keith Richards briefly escapes the Dylan oeuvre with a flash of rock and roll riffing at the bridge.

The song is one of the highlights of the *Between The Buttons* album, and is free of the muddled and murky overproduction that Jagger so dislikes. 'Who's Been Sleeping Here' also demonstrated that the Stones could draw honestly from contemporary sources without losing their own voice in the process.

COMPLICATED

Complicated' begins like a surfing track, with Charlie Watts beating out a rolling rhythm before the song erupts into a fully charged Stones pop blend, with Brian Jones playing organ. In fact, the basic sound and rhythm is virtually identical to 'My Obsession'. Dark musical textures notwithstanding, the song's content is mostly light-hearted, with the complicated, educated, sophisticated, dedicated, soft and underrated female character most likely inspired by Mick Jagger's new girlfriend Marianne Faithfull: "We talk together and discuss what is really best for us, 'cause she's so complicated." Little was Jagger aware that the complications were only beginning.

MISS AMANDA JONES

A raw electric guitar melody launches this hyped-up rock and roller. Keith Richards piles up the charged riff passages as Mick Jagger sings of Amanda Jones, a young girl from a good, wealthy family, who spends her nights at balls and discotheques, chasing good times at the risk of her own reputation. She's a party girl who maybe gets around a bit too much for her own good. "She's losing her nobility", Jagger warns. When she's not going down and down and down, young Amanda is "delightfully stoned", going up and up and up. By now in the Rolling Stones universe, young women like Amanda Jones were just another part of the scenery.

THERE MAY HAVE
BEEN SMILES FOR THE
CAMERAS BUT BRIAN
JONES WAS NOW
BEGINNING TO FRAY
AT THE EDGES.

SOMETHING HAPPENED TO ME YESTERDAY

Consider this the Stones' acid test. Their ultimate LSD freakout – *Their Satanic Majesties Request* – was still 11 months away, but 'Something Happened To Me Yesterday' was an early expression of acid fascination. Jagger and Richards sing of "something" happening, without specifically calling it acid. It's enough just knowing just how trippy, drippy and groovy the whole experience was.

The Glimmer Twins duet happily together, having a good time while parodying popular TV personality PC George Dixon (of *Dixon Of Dock Green*). The poor British bobby doesn't seem to know whether the stuff is legal or not, or even if it's right or wrong. Adding to the comedy are soaring, vaudevillian sounds made by the horns of Brian Jones, weaving a quasi-Dixieland feel on his saxophone.

The Rolling Stones would soon not be laughing quite so hard. As the authorities watched these five London boys with increasing alarm, a crackdown would soon be launched on these obnoxious troublemakers, who were already making waves with drug-references in such songs as 'Mother's Little Helper' and '19th Nervous Breakdown'. This action may seem rather strange when none of these references actually *promoted* drug use – if anything, they were grim cautionary tales – but that hardly seemed to matter now. The Rolling Stones were deemed to be enemies of society, a threat to the state. The coming years would send Jagger, Richards and Jones through a gauntlet of courtrooms and jail cells: the price to be paid by youngsters who grow too successful outside the mainstream.

THEIR SATANIC MAJESTIES REQUEST

Recorded	February to October 1967, Olympic Studios, London.
Produced by	The Rolling Stones.
Musicians	The Rolling Stones: Mick Jagger (vocals, Moog synthesizer, percussion), Brian Jones (brass, mellotron, percussion, organ, flute, recorder, electric dulcimer, saxophone, concert harp, guitar, backing vocals), Keith Richards (guitars, backing vocals), Charlie Watts (drums, percussion, tablas), Bill Wyman (bass, vocals, percussion).
	Additional personnel: Nicky Hopkins (piano, harpsichord, organ, mellotron), Eddie Kramer (percussion), Ronnie Lane (backing vocals), Steve Marriott (backing vocals and acoustic guitar), Ian Stewart (organ) John Lennon (vocals), Paul McCartney (vocals), Anita Pallenberg (vocals).

SING THIS ALL TOGETHER
CITADEL
IN ANOTHER LAND (WYMAN)
2000 MAN
SING THIS ALL TOGETHER (SEE WHAT HAPPENS)
SHE'S A RAINBOW
THE LANTERN
GOMPER
2000 LIGHT YEARS FROM HOME
ON WITH THE SHOW

DRUG ARRESTS ONLY SENT THE STONES DEEPER INTO ACID-FUELLED EXPERIMENTATION.

"So how are our two jailbirds then?" Very funny, Charlie! Weird, scary times had now come to the Rolling Stones, sending poor Mick, Keith and even fragile Brian into the angry maelstrom of a British justice system fed up with these bad boys of rock. Perhaps it was inevitable. Just how long were the proper authorities supposed to watch this loathsome quintet parade around while Andrew Loog Oldham bragged about how dangerous they were? Why lock away your virgin daughters in fear when you could lock up the Stones?

These are hard lessons for the young rock star. Not everyone is amused at the idea of fabulously wealthy, young and promiscuous delinquents thumbing their noses at their elders. At least the Beatles were discrete about such matters. Certainly Lennon and McCartney lived lives just as appalling as Jagger and Richards. And yet they'd been congratulated by the Queen, no less. But the Stones' notorious bust for "urinating in public" back in 1965 should have been clue enough that Scotland Yard was watching. The band now represented everything that was wrong with a certain troublemaking generation. And they were being made to suffer for it.

So 1967 was the year of despair. Jagger and the boys can laugh about it now, but there was nothing at all funny about the moment on February 12 when police came knocking at *Redlands*, Keith's thatched palace in West Sussex. There was a party that day, and George Harrison had just left. Now cops were marching through the door in search of illicit substances. Their first discovery was Miss Marianne Faithfull, wearing nothing but a convenient fur rug. Jagger, Richards and art dealer Robert Fraser were detained and later charged with various drug crimes: Jagger for possessing four tablets of amphetamine – bought legally in Italy; Richards for allowing pot to be smoked in his home; and Fraser for possession of heroin. All were found guilty the following June.

Jagger was sentenced to three months in jail, while Richards got one year, and Fraser six months. Bad news, to be sure. Public outcry ensued, including an influential editorial in *The Times* newspaper that questioned the severity of the sentences under the headline "Who Breaks A Butterfly On A Wheel?" After just a few days in the lockup, the Glimmer Twins were released on bail pending an appeal of their cases: not being a rock star, Fraser still had to serve four months. Meanwhile, Brian Jones was arrested on May 10 and charged with drug possession, with a trial date set for October 30. So Charlie's little wisecrack about jailbirds during the sessions for *Their Satanic Majesties Request* was no joke.

No wonder the embattled Rolling Stones were ready to escape into a lovely puddle of psychedelic mumbo-jumbo at Olympic Studios. It wasn't only escapism, but the fashion of the moment. The Beatles had just released *Sgt. Pepper's Lonely Hearts Club Band* to a stunned pop world. And Jagger didn't want to be left behind – he and Faithfull even travelled with the Beatles to North Wales to study Transcendental Meditation with the Maharishi Mahesh Yogi. The singer argued passionately with Jones and Richards that the band also needed to submerge into some drippy acid-fuelled pop. They went along with the plan, which resulted in the sonic muddle of *Their Satanic Majesties Request,* although the Stones never quite managed to escape the pressures of their lives outside the studio.

"It was made in between court sessions and lawyers with everyone sort of falling apart," Richards told *Rolling Stone* in 1971. "I ended up with chicken-pox. At the appeal, when I got up, I was covered in spots, man."

The record took almost a year to finish, as the band struggled to cope with the distractions of court dates and acid trips. Oldham was losing patience with the Stones' behaviour by then, and showed up only sporadically to "produce". What emerged were not just the usual lucrative pop tunes – although there were a few – but a collection of freakout jams. While a handful of tracks on *Their Satanic Majesties Request* are marked by a powerful grace, a good deal of the rest comes off like 'Revolution #9' out-takes, hopelessly adrift in the ether. It was an odd move for a band with its roots in the hard-edged blues of Muddy Waters. By following fashion so slavishly, the Stones recorded what is now easily their most dated album, closer in spirit to an old Seeds album than to the earth-shaking signature sound of 'Satisfaction'.

Richards admits now that the album was a shameless attempt at passing styles, a bow to the peer pressure of *Sgt. Pepper's Lonely Hearts Club Band* and too many hits of LSD. He told Kurt Loder in 1987 that he was never that interested in flower-power, though he did pay it a modicum of lip service at the time. "I am quite proud that I never did go and kiss the Maharishi's goddamn feet, you know."

The album title was not meant as a clue to the band's later interests in things satanic, but was only a play on words found in UK passports. During the making of *Their Satanic Majesties Request*, Jagger and Richards never actually slowed down long enough before the recording sessions to work out their tunes. This was their first album made away from the road and they were winging it.

"I used to defend it, but I suppose it's really indefensible," says George Chkiantz, who acted as the album's tape operator and assistant engineer. "I used to think we were the nightclub that was open after all the other nightclubs had closed. So heaps and heaps of fashionable London would appear at 3:30 or 4:00 in the morning. Which if you happen to be working at the place isn't actually what you want, thank you very much."

By the early summer, both Mick and Keith's drug charge sentences were overturned by an appeals court. Events overpowered Brian, however, and he was soon hospitalized from strain. In court during October, he admitted to possessing marijuana, but denied charges that he had cocaine and methedrine. He was found guilty, and sentenced to nine months in prison. He spent a single miserable night in a Wormwood Scrubs cell before being freed on bail, pending an appeal. The sentence was later set aside following a psychiatrist's report describing the fast-deteriorating Jones as an "extremely frightened young man" with suicidal tendencies.

The Stones had survived their most dangerous year, even if it was a far cry from Keith's deadly serious bust in Toronto in 1978, when the Mounties really did have the goods to put the guitarist away for decades. It was still enough to send poor Brian deeper into the paranoia that alienated him from the band.

Later during 1967, the Stones flew to New York City for the album's photo session. The final cover image is a silly rip-off of *Sgt. Pepper's Lonely Hearts Club Band*, with the Stones wrapped in rainbow silks, Mick wearing a sorcerer's dunce cap, and a model of Saturn hanging from the ceiling. The image originally appeared in a plastic 3-D panel glued to the album cover. Acid was clearly still the fuel of choice. "It was like being at school, you know, sticking on the coloured bits of paper and things," Jagger said in

1995 about making the cover. "It was really silly. But we enjoyed it. Also, we did it to piss Andrew off, because he was such a pain in the neck. Because he didn't understand it. The more we wanted to unload him, we decided to go on this path to alienate him."

To that end, on September 29 the Stones announced that Andrew Loog Oldham was no longer their manager or producer. He was immediately replaced as business manager by Allen Klein – a move that would have ramifications for the rest of the band's career. Producer Jimmy Miller would be recruited in time for *Beggars Banquet*, helping the Stones usher in the era of their most important work.

Not that everyone was so quick to dismiss *Their Satanic Majesties Request* – even Jagger says he still likes 'She's A Rainbow' and '2000 Light Years From Home'. It remains one of the Rolling Stones' most controversial records, for reasons not easy to explain. It stands virtually unconnected with any other Stones work, either before or after. And decades later, it remains both loved and despised.

"I thought it was a good album," says Marty Balin, singer with Jefferson Airplane. In the late-sixties, his band joined the Grateful Dead in presiding over the San Francisco psychedelic movement. Balin experienced the so-called "Summer Of Love" firsthand, drawing inspiration for an inventive blend of acid rock and tie-dyed folk.

"It was the psychedelic era, so that album was right on for me. It had that cool cover with the 3-D picture. They disowned it right away, but it's always been a favourite of many people. 'She's A Rainbow' was great, man. I still sing that to myself once in a while."

SING THIS ALL TOGETHER

Take this as a warning. The first seconds from the Rolling Stones' psychedelic opus sound like nothing their followers could have expected in 1967. Atonal banging on the piano, blasts of high-strung brass, aimless picking on the acoustic guitar. Free jazz, at last. That is soon interrupted by the pure pop vocals of Mick Jagger, leading a chorus happily through a message of peace, love and brotherhood, but the precedent has been set. Beware of noodling.

Jagger sounds relatively innocent here, as if he really, truly believed the dawn of a new age was upon us – if only we could just get our hands on the right drugs. Not that his voice has gone to mush. Mick was inherently too cynical to ever embrace anything quite so blindly, no matter how much

SHINY HAPPY PEOPLE:
THE STONES TAKE ON
PSYCHEDELIA... THE
RESULTS CONTINUE
TO POLARIZE FANS.

he wanted to believe in the hippy dream. An edge remains. He wouldn't be the first man facing prison to turn spiritual.

The track includes several layers of buzzing and clicking percussion parts, sounds which are best appreciated over a pair of headphones. Exotic and frantic, the vaguely Indian rattling is the product of Brian Jones, who also mastered the Mellotron, the harp, the saxophone, and whatever else happened to be lying around. He was the blues purist theoretically least inclined to psychedelia, except that the free-form music allowed him to experiment around the edges of songs, much as he had done on 'Paint It Black' and elsewhere. Jones may have been growing ever more estranged from the band he had founded, but he still had a crucial role within the Rolling Stones.

"The only time Brian looked like coming into his own was when they did that awful *Their Satanic Majesties Request*," Ian Stewart told Bill Wyman for his 1990 *Stone Alone* autobiography.

"It was a terrible shame... He had the ability to actually sit down and fiddle with [any musical instrument], and got something out of it very easily. The talent and ability were there, but he just screwed himself up."

While 'Sing This All Together' did not suffer from the same degree of self-indulgence as some of the other tracks, a new spaced-out vibe was obvious. The taunting, cynical tone of such earlier signature songs as the self-explanatory 'Under My Thumb' and 'Stupid Girl' was now gone.

Things were also less controlled. All that acid had clouded their judgement throughout the album, and the delicate process of weeding out the bad from the good failed them. "It's a fractured album," Richards told *Rolling Stone* in 1981. "There are some good bits, and it's weird, and there's some real crap on there as well."

CITADEL

Meaty electric guitar riffs are in short supply on *Their Satanic Majesties Request*. Where was Keef? Lost in the mix, and awash in a pool of acid and paisley. On 'Citadel', Richards asserts himself – and redeems the song – through a muscular burst of charged rhythm work. It's one of the album's few links to the Stones' rock and blues past.

The sound of 'Citadel' is otherwise charmingly dated, documenting the era's psychedelic vibe for hipster cultists and unrepentant Deadheads. Mick's unique edge is blunted and relaxed, as if trapped within the lethargic conventions of a limited genre. And as he serenades a mysterious "Candy and Cathy" with glancing social commentary – "Flags are flying dollar bills, from the heights of concrete hills" – he could just as easily be singing about incense and peppermints.

Critic Robert Palmer has suggested that 'Citadel' was one of a number of tracks on the album that inadvertently encouraged the unfortunate excesses of progressive rock. If so, bands such as Yes and the bombastic Emerson, Lake and Palmer overlooked one crucial point: not even the Stones took this seriously.

IN ANOTHER LAND

The quietest Stone speaks. The Rolling Stones had already declared "it's the singer, not the song" to the world. Now Bill Wyman was about to test that philosophy with 'In Another Land', the bassist's only lead vocal and songwriting credit on a legitimate Rolling Stones album. Here was further indication of just how distracted Jagger and Richards had become by the outside world.

THEIR SATANIC MAJESTIES REQUEST

Wyman, Watts and pianist Nicky Hopkins arrived on schedule for a session at Olympic Studios on July 13, only to discover that the Jagger and Richards would not be attending. With costly studio time already blocked out, engineer Glyn Johns asked Wyman if he had a song to record. What Wyman had was something he had just written on his organ at home. The working title was, fittingly, 'Acid In The Grass'.

On the final version of 'In Another Land', Wyman sings of a romantic, dreamlike encounter of uncertain meaning. His flat delivery is drowned beneath a thick layer of tremolo and Hopkins' genteel harpsichord melodies. Consequently, Wyman doesn't try very hard to emote. The Small Faces were working next door, so singer Steve

BILL WYMAN MADE HIS COMPOSITIONAL DEBUT WHEN THE GLIMMER TWINS FAILED TO MAKE IT TO THE STUDIO.

Marriott was invited to help out with the vocals.

"A lot of people were meandering around the studio," says Chkaintz. "A lot of groups – and the Faces were certainly one of them – were either doing a session in the other studio or had just finished or were thinking about starting."

At the next day's Stones session, Mick and Keith were played the tape of 'In Another Land'. The sweet waves of melody were clearly right for the album. They both agreed, and overdubbed some additional background vocals on to the recording. Mick's voice erupts during the chorus, adding a much-needed spark of energy to the pop ballad – "Then I awoke, was this some kind of joke?" The snoring that closes the track is Wyman's.

The Jagger/Richards songwriting monopoly was broken – even if failed permanently to alter a situation that Wyman often found creatively frustrating. He wasn't alone. Although he'd started the band, Brian Jones had been continually shut out. Jagger even went as far as to say of him: "I've never known a guy with less talent for songwriting." In later years, Mick Taylor – Jones' replacement – reportedly quit the Stones because he was not receiving the songwriting credit he felt was deserved.

Wyman eventually found his own outlet, embarking on the most prolific solo career of the original Stones. He recorded two solo albums in the 1970s – *Monkey Grip* and *Stone Alone* – enjoyed a major international hit single in 1981 with '(Si Si) Je Suis Un Rock Star', and, in 1985, released an album of early rock and roll credited to Willie and the Poor Boys – a band that included Wyman, Watts, Ringo Starr, Jimmy Page of Led Zeppelin and vocalist Paul Rodgers of Free and Bad Company. In spite of this, to most fans of the Stones the spacey 'In Another Land' remains Wyman's best-known recording.

"It came out because it seemed to work with the rest of the songs on the album," Wyman told *Guitar Player* magazine in 1978. "But you have to look on it as a complete coincidence. I mean, if everybody had turned up that night, that song never would have appeared on record. That's the way it is."

2000 MAN

Mick Jagger is no prophet, but even at the age of 23 the singer was wise enough to understand that generational conflict was nothing new, and wouldn't end with the 1960s generation. In '2000 Man', Jagger looks to the future and predicts the same gaps – "My kids, they just don't understand me at all".

He could have been referring to a destiny that both he and his own peers would have to face in coming decades. The song also questions what lasting legacy his era would leave. "Oh, daddy, is your brain still flashing like it did when you were young? Or did it come down crashing, seeing all the things you done?" These are serious considerations for a rock god who would by the 1990s be older than both the British Prime Minister and the President of the United States.

A crisp acoustic guitar pattern guides '2000 Man', blending into waves of organ, as the song repeatedly shifts gears and tempos. And why not? By the 1967 sessions, the Stones were a tight unit. They may have stopped touring in 1966, but with the likely exception of Brian Jones, drugs hadn't yet affected their chops.

Keith Richards can often now be heard talking with reverence of the mighty Charlie Watts, who he credits for much of the Stones' muscle. While the rhythm section of Watts and Wyman has come to enjoy a reputation of near-mythic proportions, their role was less clear back in the prickly, sensitive days of *Their Satanic Majesties Request*. Mick may have been reaching for a

THE COOLEST MAN IN THE WORLD: CHARLIE WATTS OBSERVES THE MADNESS OF PSYCHEDELIA AND DRUG BUSTS

sixties utopia, but he and Richards were a bit high-strung from being in and out of courtrooms and jail cells.

That was clear the day Watts made a rare suggestion in the studio. Andy Johns, who later worked with the Stones between 1969 and 1974, remembers visiting the sessions engineered by his brother Glyn, and seeing "Mick and Keith fall over laughing that Charlie had made a suggestion. Mick put the talkback button down, laughing, so everyone could hear him: 'Keith ha-ha-ha! Charlie just made a suggestion!' It was a little mean."

Over the years, Watts assumed a more important position. His opinion mattered, particularly on the choice of the bassists who would join the band after Wyman retired in 1993.

"They didn't really use to listen to what old Charlie had to say, and they would run him through the ringer on drum parts all the time," says Johns. "Some of those drum parts on the earlier records are really unusual."

Watts often seems to have viewed the Stones as if were just his job. As he once told the teenaged Johns, "You don't think I take this seriously, do you? It's just a fucking rock and roll band."

SING THIS ALL TOGETHER (SEE WHAT HAPPENS)

Here is where *Their Satanic Majesties Request* veers off into aimless noodling. Here the Stones try to push the musical envelope beyond where the Beatles and the Beach Boys last left it. But in the context of the Stones' oevre, of the band's strengths and lasting importance, this eight-minute free-for-all is practically an embarrassment. A bad trip.

Improvisation was never the Stones' mission. And yet on this reprise of the album's opening track, Keith and the others jam to no discernible conclusion. The "song" opens with giggling and chatter from the left speaker, and the comment, "Where's that joint?" Where indeed? What follows is a gurgling of brass, bells and whistles, during which Mick works hard at his chanting, moaning and heavy breathing. In a moment, Jagger's vocals suddenly find clarity through the song's central melody.

'Sing This All Together (See What Happens)' is not without some charm. It at least represents a period where they were not locked into the hard-rock mould that would carry them from the 1970s through the 1990s. But there's no plan, and the song is ultimately unsatisfying.

The overall failure of *Their Satanic Majesties Request* should not suggest that the Stones had lost touch with their central talents. George Chkaintz remembers being directed by engineer Glyn Johns to fetch a new reel of tape from the Olympic Studios store. He took a shortcut through Studio B. "That was a time when there were just oodles of people – hangers on, Beatles, various and so on," Chkaintz says now. "I hurried through this room, which was full of people, and Keith is playing a little white Hammond organ, which belonged to one of the advertising geezers who used the studio. And he was just tapping it rhythmically, not really playing any kind of tune; it was all to do with rhythm. I must have got about two-thirds of the way down the room, and I got frozen. It was fascinating, I just got caught by this thing."

When Glyn impatiently came looking for his tape operator, he too was hypnotized by Keith's organ recital. "The quality of his rhythm I've always found exceptional anyway," Chkaintz says. "But this wasn't from his instrument or anything. It was just mesmerizing. It's important to realize that you were dealing with people of that calibre, who just could do it in a way that very few others can."

THE STONES FAILED TO REACH THE BENCHMARKS OF PSYCHEDELIA ALREADY CREATED BY THE BEATLES.

SHE'S A RAINBOW

The world's greatest pop band? No one ever made that claim for the Rolling Stones. Pop was for nice people, not those shaggy anti-Beatles from London. But by the mid-sixties, pop had become the Stones' language of choice. Even if they had rockers ('Satisfaction') and R&B covers ('Time Is On My Side') at their disposal, the Stones mastered the frazzled pop melody long before the drug-addled menace of *Exile On Main Street* took hold. This was the era between the Rolling Stones' days as blues purists and their later years as the masters of hard rock and roll.

'She's A Rainbow' was the final pure pop moment for the Stones. It was the last time Mick Jagger would ever sound child-like, singing fairy tale lyrics utterly devoid of his usual sex-baiting cynicism. The irony here is that the album's most accessible pop track rises from the depths of a brief, but grating introduction of pre-industrial electronic moaning, scraping and found dialogue. Then out pops a blissful piano melody and a regal blast of horns fit enough for Buckingham Palace.

"Have you seen her dressed in blue?" sings Jagger with almost heartbreaking innocence. If the rest of the album had been of this calibre, even the Beatles would have been worried. No acid necessary. The soft, euphoric textures owe a good deal to the presence of strings, arranged by John Paul Jones, destined two years later to play bass with Led Zeppelin. Jones was a regular presence at Olympic. He found work in a variety of genres, much as his future bandmate, guitar deity Jimmy Page, paid his rent with session work for the Kinks, Marianne Faithfull and others.

"John Paul Jones did quite a lot of session work," says George Chkiantz, who also engineered for Led Zeppelin. "Olympic was a sound stage for quite a lot of films, not to mention all the jingle work we did as well. We met John Paul Jones in that capacity quite often."

THE LANTERN

An experiment in stereophonic sound, 'The Lantern' offers the album's strangest, most barren, and jumbled mixture of elements. The creamy background vocals and Keith's rocking riffing erupt from nowhere, and then disappear again just as quickly. A horn section drones loudly, and Mick sings with some restraint, performing enigmatic lyrics in a dreamy mood. It's a story fit for Edgar Allen Poe – "My face, it turns a deathly pale, you're talking to me through your veil".

Nonetheless, the track contains a link to the rock and country sounds at the Stones' deepest roots, most notable within the sudden, ecstatic flashes of guitar. Even amidst the swirling chaos, 'The Lantern' rocks, but only in frustrating spurts. In many ways it is like much of *Their Satanic Majesties Request*, offering many fine moments, mixed in with a collection of ill-conceived or unfinished ideas.

"It had interesting things on it, but I don't think any of the songs are very good." This was Jagger's final verdict delivered to *Rolling Stone* magazine in 1995. "It's a bit like *Between The Buttons*. It's a sound experience, really, rather than a song experience."

GOMPER

Watch now as the Stones try very hard to become George Harrison. Their own *Sgt. Pepper's Lonely Hearts Club Band* would be incomplete without it. 'Gomper' is largely a throwaway, hardly a "song" at all, though it's buoyed with a dazzling array of exotic percussion by Brian Jones. The track begins and ends within an Indian-influenced rhythmic pattern, making sudden shifts into pop, rather like Harrison's 'Within You Without You'.

'Gomper' is one of the album's most deeply psychedelic excursions, but the ultimate result is disjointed and derivative. The Stones had already discovered the dynamic instrumentation of North Africa for themselves, but Jagger even sings a bit like Beatle George on 'Gomper', painting an idyllic picture of a woman communing with nature. Most satisfying, Jones' percussion work suggests that he might have re-emerged as a force within the Stones if only he'd been healthy and clear-headed enough.

"I THOUGHT IT WAS A GOOD ALBUM... THEY DISOWNED IT RIGHT AWAY, BUT IT'S ALWAYS BEEN A FAVOURITE OF MINE."
MARTY BALIN, JEFFERSON AIRPLANE

2000 LIGHT YEARS FROM HOME

Before the Rolling Stones resurrected this dark, swirling pop number for their 1989 Steel Wheels tour, it was just another forgotten track from an album few cared to remember. Hardcore Stones fans always understood its charms. However, the Stones' larger-than-life performance on a multi-million-dollar stage gave new life to a song that is now widely seen as one of the highlights of the psychedelic era.

The track unfolds into a wave of drifting, spacey instrumentation, creeping slowly into the twilight zone. A rumbling beat from Charlie Watts mingles with a guitar riff resembling one of Ennio Morricone's spaghetti western themes. And Jagger sings of interplanetary isolation, perhaps inspired by his few days in jail. Helping bring the tune to life is Brian Jones, making sense of those dreamy Mellotron sounds.

"That was one of the great space songs," says Marty Balin of Jefferson Airplane. "We were into that kind of stuff, too. When I first heard that I loved it. The sounds on there were real unique. I think a good song can be done in any field by anybody. Anybody could do '2000 Light Years From Home'. It wouldn't sound like the Stones, but it would translate for anyone, because you could identify with what he was talking about, and with the funky keys."

Like the rest of *Their Satanic Majesties Request*, the science-fiction epic was recorded on to the Olympic four-track machine, no more complicated than any other Stones track. Repeat echo effects, and thuds and thumps from an orchestral bass drum that was laying around the studio were slowed down and later added to the basic track.

"When it came to the overdubs all hell was let loose. We just tried anything and everything," says Chkiantz. "It was all basically conventional recording. We tried to do funny things with vocals and make funny sounds with various bits and bobs, and most of them got left off in the end."

ON WITH THE SHOW

On With The Show' is the album's most playful track. It opens with the sidewalk pitch of a gentleman barker working to draw customers in to see his naked girlie show. Keith Richards snaps out a sharp little guitar lick, and Jagger announces that "Bettina starts her show at two o'clock."

What follows are Jagger's lyrics of burlesque humour, made frenetic through layers of percussion and other bits and pieces added by Brian Jones, before an inevitable finale and some heated cocktail party chatter.

The song is rather light-hearted for a band that would be singing songs about Lucifer and fighting in the streets in just a matter of months, and that coming transformation would spark the band's most important work. In 1967, however, escapism was inevitable, even if the promised prison terms awaiting Mick, Keith and Brian never materialized. If not for those gnawing distractions of the law, the Stones just might have pulled off a more consistent psychedelic exploration. Even so, *Their Satanic Majesties Request* climbed the charts to No. 3 in the UK, and No. 2 in the US.

"It was a very self-indulgent mess in many ways," Chkiantz says. "But it's very difficult for me to hear *Their Satanic Majesties Request* without getting the smells and colours of the room back. I quite like it, but that doesn't mean it's good."

BEGGARS BANQUET

Recorded	March to July 1968, Olympic Studios, London.
Produced by	Jimmy Miller.
Musicians	The Rolling Stones: Mick Jagger (vocals, harmonica), Brian Jones (slide guitar, backing vocals, sitar, tamboura, mellotron, harmonica), Keith Richards (acoustic and electric guitar, bass guitar, lead, backing vocals), Charlie Watts (drums, percussion, backing vocals), Bill Wyman (bass guitar, backing vocals, percussion). Additional musicians: Rocky Dijon (congas), Ric Grech (fiddle), Nicky Hopkins (piano), Dave Mason (Mellotron, shehnai), Jimmy Miller (backing vocals), Watts Street Gospel Choir (backing vocals).

SYMPATHY FOR THE DEVIL
NO EXPECTATIONS
DEAR DOCTOR
PARACHUTE WOMAN
JIG-SAW PUZZLE
STREET FIGHTING MAN
PRODIGAL SON (WILKINS)
STRAY CAT BLUES
FACTORY GIRL
SALT OF THE EARTH

FRENCH AVANT-
GARDE FILM
MAKER JEAN-LUC
GODARD *(CENTRE)*
DOCUMENTED THE
RECORDING OF
'SYMPATHY FOR
THE DEVIL'.

The Rolling Stones found their moment of absolute clarity in 1968, after a long season of drug busts, bad press, and that swirl of forced experimentation called *Their Satanic Majesties Request*. Confusion was replaced by a new sense of purpose, where passing psychedelic fashion was cast aside in favour of the blues and rock roots that had first inspired them. Here was a band back in control of its destiny.

Beggars Banquet emerged from a brief period of relative calm. Not that there weren't the usual moments of high misadventure. The early morning album sessions at Olympic Studios were interrupted on June 11 when fire engines were called out to extinguish a blaze ignited by a faulty arc lamp hung from the ceiling. It had been put there by one of the film crew working on Jean-Luc Godard's *One Plus One*, a film that inadvertently documented the recording of 'Sympathy For The Devil'. By the time the fire crews left, much of the band's equipment was soaked, but the Stones were back at work the next morning.

While the band's legal problems were not yet completely behind them, there was no longer the feeling of impending doom that had clouded the previous year. Mick Jagger was actually enjoying a relatively quiet life with Marianne Faithfull in a rented house in London's Chester Square, spending his days reading poetry and philosophy. "It was a wonderful time," Faithfull says now of that era. "The biggest thing in the air was love."

Faithfull was involved in the theatre, and had just finished work on the X-rated art film *Girl On A Motorcycle*. Both were mingling happily with a young crowd of stage directors, film-makers and gallery owner Robert Fraser's hipster art crowd. "I wasn't taking so many drugs that it was messing up my creative processes," Jagger told *Rolling Stone* in 1995. "It was a very good period, 1968 – there was a good feeling in the air. It was a very creative period for everyone."

The result was not just a haunting new rock sound a la 'Sympathy For The Devil', but a rustic country flavour already being explored on Bob Dylan's *John Wesley Harding* and the Byrds' *Sweetheart Of The Rodeo*. Richards' renewed interest put the Stones squarely within that movement, with compelling results. The band had rarely before approached the scratchy authenticity now on display in their rendition of the Reverend Robert Wilkins' 'Prodigal Son', sung by Jagger on *Beggars Banquet* in a nervous, twangy warble. The Stones were finally tapping into the soul of their beloved blues in a way their early cover versions had never quite managed. Likewise, Jagger sounded more nasty, amused and dangerous than ever in the torrid opening seconds of 'Stray Cat Blues'.

Beggars Banquet also marked the final meaningful contribution from the rapidly fading Brian Jones, who emerged from his wounded stupor long enough to provide elegant slide guitar work on 'No Expectations' and elsewhere. Jones' relationship with actress Anita Pallenberg had ended in Morocco, where she had taken up with Keith Richards. But his slide playing could still generate the same shivers of emotion Mick and Keith first encountered when Elmo Lewis – as Jones had once liked to be known – played his earliest licks at the Ealing and Marquee clubs. "Brian was absolutely brilliant when he was on form, remembers George Chkiantz, who worked as assistant engineer on Beggars Banquet. "The trouble is that when he wasn't on form, it was not to be borne easily."

Producer Jimmy Miller was brought into the Stones fold early in the sessions, beginning a collaboration that would last until 1973. During those years, Miller and the Stones would record some of the most powerful albums in the history of the genre – *Beggars Banquet*, *Let It Bleed*, *Sticky Fingers* and *Exile On Main Street*. Jagger recruited Miller after hearing his work with Traffic. The American-born producer arrived just as the Stones were finding a new hardened flair in their sound, as demonstrated in their very first project together, the single 'Jumpin' Jack Flash' – introduced to television viewers via an alarming film clip of the band vamping in war paint, with both Jones and Richards wearing bug-eyed shades.

"You get someone like Jimmy, who can turn the whole band on, make a nondescript number into something, which is what happened on *Beggars*

"IT WAS A VERY GOOD PERIOD, 1968 – THERE WAS A GOOD FEELING IN THE AIR. IT WAS A VERY CREATIVE PERIOD FOR EVERYONE."

MICK JAGGER

Banquet," Richards told *Crawdaddy* magazine in 1975. "We were just coming out of *Satanic Majesties*... Mick was making movies, everything was on the point of dispersal. I had nicked Brian's old lady. It was a mess. And Jimmy pulled *Beggars Banquet* out of all that."

If the Stones' provocative new interest in all things Satanic was ultimately a put-on, it suited the dark times that were coming. Swinging London, flower power, the Beach Boys' 'Good Vibrations' were beginning to fade in a new season of political assassinations, calls for revolution and the deepening morass of the Vietnam War. 'All You Need Is Love' no longer seemed appropriate. Any rock act hoping to be taken seriously by the increasingly troubled youth culture marching in the streets was required to deal in some way with the new socio-political rumblings of the era. The Beatles responded with 'Helter Skelter' and 'Revolution'. The Stones, already feared by parents and the proper authorities as the bad boys of British rock, could do no less.

Jagger was well-suited to the role of provocateur, inspired by many of the same works of literature and old blues recordings that lit a fire beneath the Doors in Los Angeles. While Jagger's new persona was the demonic gentleman, Jim Morrison sang of explosive journeys into hedonism and rebellion, following a troubled psyche to apocalyptic confrontations with the ruling generation. According to Ray Manzarek, organist with the Doors, the desire to explore man's darker impulses – an approach they shared with the Stones – came from "knowing that the other side of life is death, and you better dance madly".

As ever, Manzarek says, the experience of black America provided an alarming resource. "The idea that you are going to die infuses your life with a depth and a meaning, which is why the blues were so powerful. As a black man in America – not so much in the fifties but in the earlier years – you could be hung at any moment. They would hang you, or they would harass you, they would cut you, they would shoot you down. So walking the streets of white America as a black man was always a matter of life and death."

Jagger was happy to be the bearer of bad news, but he was no activist or working-class hero. He would never hold a press conference with Yippie leader Jerry Rubin or any other political gadfly. Better to let Lennon play that game. After Jagger's drug conviction was overturned following an appeal, the singer was interviewed live on UK television as a reluctant spokesman for his generation. The habits that had brought him so much trouble, he declared, were simply "a matter of one's own private life", not a revolutionary act.

A more pressing issue was the launch of *Beggars Banquet*, unexpectedly stalled when both Decca in England and London Records in the US refused to release it with the intended cover art. As originally designed, the cover was a photograph of a bathroom wall and toilet covered in graffiti. For nearly four months, the Stones refused to discuss changing the design, before finally agreeing to release the album with a simple white cover – in spite of an unfortunate resemblance to the Beatles' "White Album". The original *Beggars Banquet* cover would not see the light of day until the 1980s.

During the delay, Jagger began work on the film *Performance*, starring alongside Anita Pallenberg in a psychodrama directed by Donald Cammell and Nicolas Roeg. He returned in time to celebrate the album's release with a Stones food-fight during a press conference at London's Kensington Gore Hotel.

The band, however, was not prepared to tour in 1968. The very idea of rehashing the old hits was now a profoundly uninteresting idea to Jagger. "People say that audiences are listening now, but to what? Like the Rolling Stones on stage isn't the Boston Pops Symphony Orchestra. It's a load of noise," Jagger said in 1968. "On record it can be quite musical, but when you get to the stage it's no virtuoso performance. It's a rock and roll act, a very good one, and nothing more."

SYMPATHY FOR THE DEVIL

Enter Lucifer. Not as a way of life, nor even as a partner in crime, but as a telling metaphor for the dark side of the human soul. Here was the ultimate outlaw anthem, an expression of the danger and dread that Andrew Loog Oldham had long promoted as being the band's mission. Maybe Robert Johnson sold his soul to the Devil in return for his supernatural chops, but Mick Jagger's exploration of the satanic was for his own ends, not for anyone else. Jagger was inspired to write 'Sympathy For The Devil' after Faithfull had given him a copy of Mikhail Bulgakov's *The Master And Margarita*. The book features the Devil as its debonair central character, the host of a fabulous ball in Moscow, and a master of high society. Jagger's reaction was a challenge to mainstream values, depicting Satan in the song not as a terrible beast, but as a sophisticated "man of wealth and taste", a role the singer embraced.

His phrasing is vaguely Dylanesque, but more agitated, even confrontational across the song's relentless samba beat. The lyrics travel through dark moments from history – the Crucifixion, the Russian revolution, World War II – before putting a new spin on recent events. It was a notable accomplishment, even within an epic six-minute pop song. Jagger's suggestion that "it was you and me" who killed the Kennedys is a provocative and memorable line, even if its implications are less than clear. More disturbing is an unsettling use of role-reversal, disrupting the accepted rules of society. "Every cop is a criminal," he warns, "and all the sinners saints".

The persona Jagger created with 'Sympathy For The Devil' was so effective that it would haunt the band for years, causing some fans to abandon them in fear. Suspicions on Jagger's true motives only intensified after the blood-soaked disaster of 1969's free concert at Altamont Speedway. But Faithfull called the song "pure papier-mache Satanism" in her 1994 autobiography. And Jagger says he never intended the song as an endorsement of black magic, nor as an inspiration to the laughable brand of satanic metal that emerged in the seventies and eighties. "The satanic imagery stuff was very overplayed," Jagger said in 1995. "We didn't want to really go down that road. And I felt that song was enough. You didn't want to make a career out of it."

"IT'S A ROCK AND ROLL ACT, A VERY GOOD ONE, AND NOTHING MORE."
MICK JAGGER

But for Keith Richards, at least, this dance with the devil seemed less a metaphor than a new hobby. Both he and Anita dabbled in the black arts, and seemed to actively encourage others to do the same. "It's something everybody ought to explore. There are possibilities there," Richards told *Rolling Stone* magazine in 1971. "Why do people practice voodoo? All these things bunged under the name of superstition and old wives' tales. I'm no expert in it… I just try to bring it into the open a little. When we were just innocent kids out for a good time, they were saying 'They're evil, they're evil.' Oh, I'm evil, really? So that makes you start thinking about evil."

The metamorphosis of 'Sympathy For The Devil' from a simple folk ballad into its final state as a hypnotic rocker is well documented, thanks to the fortuitous presence of Jean-Luc Godard's *One Plus One* cameras at Olympic. "Godard happened to catch us on two very good nights," Jagger said in 1968. "He might have come every night for two weeks and just seen us looking at each other with blank faces."

In the film – which mingles the tedious in-studio shots of the Stones with absurd scenes of black poet revolutionaries loudly worshipping white women – the song slowly takes shape as Jagger, Richards and Jones slowly strum acoustic guitars. Richards is later seen playing bass, as Wyman

77

performs percussion alongside Watts and Rocky Dijon. The finished track also includes rare straight-ahead lead guitar playing by Richards, who patches together a progression of stinging notes that is occasionally awkward, but always exciting.

"'Sympathy For The Devil' was a nightmare from start to end," George Chkiantz says with a laugh. "It went on for several days. There was all the film crew mucking around in it. The song changed out of all recognition, from one end to the other. You could see a development and it was quite interesting, and it was very tiring."

The lengthy sessions were nothing unusual for the Stones, who would often enter the studio unrehearsed, with only the barest sketch of a song prepared. "There were loads of people that said this method was super expensive for no good purpose. But I don't think that's actually true. Jagger really felt that unless you had gone through it until nobody could stand it anymore you didn't purify the material. The record companies don't like that, when they're paying the bills. The curious thing is that I can scarcely remember anything of the earlier takes, which makes me feel they got the best track."

NO EXPECTATIONS

Witness the vagabond blues, as true for the Willy Lomans of the road as for the anonymous bands of young men making music in one town after another. 'No Expectations' is a tender acceptance of that life on the road, where love is likely to be a fleeting experience at best, and long-term commitment an impossibility.

The sound on 'No Expextations' is elegant and raw, just the quiet strumming of acoustic guitars, while Brian Jones creates a moving passage of bottleneck guitar right out of the Mississippi Delta. "Our love is like our music," Jagger sings regretfully, as if forever en route to some airport, train station or highway. "It's here and then it's gone."

The track was recorded at Olympic Studios in London with the band gathered in a circle, singing and playing into open microphones. The track also marked one of Jones' last flashes of brilliance on a Rolling Stones recording. By now, drugs, paranoia and fading health were pulling him away from the muse that had once inspired him and given him the energy to launch the Rollin' Stones. But 'No Expectations' showed that Jones was still capable of producing deeply moving instrumental flourishes. "That

A FRIENDSHIP WAS SHATTERED WHEN ANITA PALLENBERG LEFT BRIAN JONES FOR KEITH RICHARDS.

was the last time I remember Brian really being totally involved in something that was really worth doing," Jagger told *Rolling Stone* magazine in 1995. "He had just lost interest in everything."

Not quite everything, however. Jones would periodically emerge from his cloud to demonstrate a continued interest in creating music, and in exploring new ideas. While the Rolling Stones impatiently awaited the release of *Beggars Banquet* in 1968, Jones travelled to Morocco that July to record the Master Musicians of Joujouka, whose soulful trance rhythms had captured his excited imagination. Jones was introduced to this family of players in the hills south of Tangier by expatriate writer Brion Gysin. Engineer George Chkiantz was soon summoned from Olympic for the recording.

"My plane arrived at 9 o'clock in the morning," Chkiantz recalls now. "The Stones office asked me to phone him up – 'Brian says he'll meet you. If he does, give us a ring because nobody will believe that he's going to be anywhere at 9 o'clock in the morning.' But he was. He was there."

Even more surprising was Jones' demeanour during this period. "He was the most extraordinarily together person there, in Joujouka, up in the hills. Not when he got back to Tangiers. Different story," says Chkiantz. "In Joujouka he was extraordinary."

Jones had travelled to North Africa with his new girlfriend Suki Potier, and quickly slid back into his addictions once he returned from the hills. At one point he collapsed on the balcony of his Tangier hotel room. But Jones never lost his obsession with the Joujouka project. After three days of work, Chkiantz happily stumbled back into his room at the Es Saadi Hotel and collapsed, only to be summoned again by Jones. "I remember being woke up by Brian saying he couldn't get the tape recorder to work," Chkiantz says. "So half in my sleep I sort of stormed out, waggled some connection, pressed a play button and said 'There, see,' and went back to bed. To my great embarrassment I remember having no clothes on at all. I have no idea who was in the room. I remember apologizing to Suki afterwards."

The final result of Jones' last great enthusiasm wouldn't emerge until 1971, when *Brian Jones Presents The Pipes Of Pan* was finally released on Rolling Stones Records. It wasn't exactly music for the pop masses, but Jones' foray into the hills of Morocco would have ramifications as late as 1989. That's when Jagger and Richards returned to the village of JouJouka during work on *Steel Wheels* to weave some of those hypnotic rhythms into the Rolling Stones' sound via 'Continental Drift'.

DEAR DOCTOR

Country music was nothing new to the Rolling Stones. Back in 1964, the band recorded a hyped-up rendition of Hank Snow's 'I'm Moving On'. But the Beggars Banquet sessions suggested a deepening interest in the universal torch and twang of the redneck waltz, which already shared a surface accent with the Stones' beloved deep blues. With 'Dear Doctor', these London rockers sounded about ready for the Southern honky tonk circuit, appropriating yet another American pop style.

"Keith has always been country," Jagger told *Rolling Stone* magazine in 1968. His earliest memory of Richards is that of a toddler dressed like Roy Rogers. "That's what his scene was. We still think of country songs as a bit of a joke, I'm afraid. We don't really know anything about country music really. We're just playing games. We aren't really into it enough to know."

On 'Dear Doctor', Jagger sings as a confused young man overcome with doubt on his wedding day. "Oh the gal I'm to marry is a bowlegged sow," Jagger moans. "I've been soaking up drink like a sponge." His voice is embraced by a warm blend of acoustic guitars and harmonica as Jagger's groom is relieved to discover he's been jilted by his bride.

This isn't country music, not yet. Look forward a few years to the terrible torture and twang of *Exile On Main Street*. What we have in *Beggars Banquet* is straight-ahead rock, played by the absolute masters of the form with an occasional folk spin or southern warble. And if this comical vignette is less than a respectful tribute to the world of Hank Williams and Merle Haggard, then 'Dear Doctor' at least showed the Stones could get the sound right. For that, they owe a debt to the influence to two other albums released in 1968: Bob Dylan's *John Wesley Harding* and the Byrds' *Sweetheart Of The Rodeo*. Both were country-flavoured milestones, and Jagger acknowledges their impact on *Beggars Banquet*.

Following his 1966 motorcycle accident, Dylan embarked on an introspective trek into country-flavoured rock and folk music. The Byrds, meanwhile, had recruited new keyboardist Gram Parsons, who immediately began lobbying bandleader Roger McGuinn to record a full country album. The Byrds had already dabbled in bluegrass and country by then, so McGuinn agreed. "It was just a coincidence," remembers McGuinn. "We really had no contact with Bob Dylan at that point It was after his motorcycle wreck and he was up in Woodstock recuperating, and evidently writing country songs. We didn't know it until we asked for some material

"MAYBE IT WAS TIME TO GET LAID BACK BECAUSE THINGS HAD BEEN SO INTENSE WITH THE PSYCHEDELIC ERA."
ROGER MCGUINN, THE BYRDS

81

from Bob, as we did periodically to see what he was up to. We got 'You Ain't Going Nowhere,' and it was obviously a country song. It's really one of those nebulous, almost mystical things. It was something that affected a lot of people independently in different parts of the globe at the same time. Maybe it was time to get laid back because things had been so intense with the psychedelic era."

On *Sweetheart Of The Rodeo*, there was none of the Stones' playful disrespect for the country genre or its audience. It had been a faithful attempt at the heartfelt sounds Parsons knew from his George Jones and Porter Wagner records. The Byrds even travelled to that Taj Mahal of country music – the Grand Ole Opry in Nashville, where this band of West Coast hippies was greeted by tepid applause. Soon, Parsons was urging McGuinn to hire a steel-guitar player and permanently transform the Byrds into a full-time country act. McGuinn wasn't interested, so Parsons and bassist Chris Hillman left to form the Flying Burrito Brothers.

Three decades later, *Sweetheart…* remains deeply influential, helping inspire a new generation of country rock bands, epitomized by Wilco and Son Volt. And the reputation of Parsons, who became a close friend to Keith Richards before his death in 1973, has since grown to legendary proportions. "He was a colourful character," McGuinn says. "We had a lot of fun together. We used play pool, ride motorcycles and drink beer together. I just know him as a picker. I don't see him as James Dean."

When McGuinn heard the new country flavours of *Beggars Banquet*, it somehow made sense. "I knew Gram was hanging out with Mick and Keith in London," McGuinn says, "so it didn't surprise me too much."

PARACHUTE WOMAN

Old blues metaphors are drafted into this seething expression of young lust from a heavy breathing Mick Jagger. He delivers his message with lascivious glee, rolling his tongue around lyrics of coarse sexual innuendo that would have a hard time getting past would-be censors if released today – "My heavy throbber's itchin' just to lay a solo rhythm down."

Jagger is joined by a roaring harp finale and one of Jones' harshest passages of slide guitar. Beneath it all is a low rumble the Stones created by recording a rhythm track on a simple mono cassette recorder, much to the astonishment of the recording engineers at Olympic. "They fell in love with the sound of this thing," says Chkiantz. "If you got the distortion just about right it had a curious kind of warble, which was a remarkably gutsy sound."

The band would gather around the cassette recorder, armed with instruments suited to the machine: Bill Wyman on a fretless acoustic bass guitar; Charlie Watts pounding a street drummer's kit; Jagger on percussion; Richards on acoustic guitar; Jones on various instruments, including sitar. Once completed, the cassette track would be added to the studio four-track machine, to be overdubbed by another electric track.

"That was really fascinating. It worked incredibly well," says Chkiantz. "The Stones, never known for efficient and quick work, were actually in serious threat of getting more than a track done in a night, rather than one track in seven days."

Elsewhere on the album, 'Street Fighting Man' owes Jones' sitar-playing to the same lo-fi process. "It twangs away," Richards said in 1971. " He's holding notes that wouldn't come through if you had a board, you wouldn't be able to fit it in. That was really an electronic track, up in the realms... It's nice to make it simpler sometimes."

'JIGSAW PUZZLE' WAS AMONG THE MOST DYLAN-INFLUENCED OF SONGS BY THE ROLLING STONES.

83

JIGSAW PUZZLE

Not even Mick Jagger could escape the influence of the mighty Bob Dylan, that high priest of meaning in 1960s pop music. Neither could the likes of Lennon and McCartney. But even the devil himself must eventually succumb to the word according to Saint Bob, which helps explain 'Jigsaw Puzzle', with its lyrics loaded with clever detail, and Jagger's unusually flat but determined delivery.

"He was like the big guy that you all looked up to," says Roger McGuinn of the Byrds, a band that recorded several of Dylan's songs. "Even McCartney says that. Everybody was looking up to Dylan the way people would read Kerouac. He was the person with the most to say, with the greatest amount of artistic integrity. He really did represent the whole generation. So we all listened to what Bob was doing, and it trickled down."

Jagger could at least rest in peace knowing that he would never suffer that unfortunate label – "The New Dylan". On 'Jigsaw Puzzle', Jagger almost sounds uncomfortable with all these words, as if he really could express more with less – like the great bluesmen who had been such an influence on the Stones. Jagger has never been overly fond of the song, although it would be a mistake to ignore its strengths, such as the rumbling slide guitar licks. Meanwhile, Jagger sings a wry description of a band much like his own whose "singer looks so angry at being thrown to the lions".

STREET FIGHTING MAN

Mick Jagger is no revolutionary. Make no mistake, for all the mainstream anger against long hair and funny clothes, the Glimmer Twins were never out to destroy you and "your petty morals", as young Keith once described them. The only jail time the Stones ever suffered was for illicit drugs. Hardly the stuff of revolution. Even David Crosby and James Brown were busted on weapons charges. But if things were quiet at home in London, there was serious trouble brewing in Paris and America, where questions about the Vietnam War, free speech and civil rights, brought young people on to the streets. Jagger understood the inherent passion behind such an impulse, enough to make one of the most unexpectedly meaningful statements of the era.

If Dylan was then the essential voice of protest in pop music, the Rolling Stones at least emerged ready to step into the fray, if only long enough to check out the scene. "Summer's here and the time is right for fighting in the streets," Jagger sings in a tone of urgency and near-confusion. "What else can a poor boy do 'cept sing in a rock and roll band?"

Here was a taunting note of ambivalence that suggested the Rolling Stones had given more thought to the day's events and their consequences than a thousand bands of beaded, bearded hippies screaming "Up against the wall, motherfuckers!" They may have craved a certain hedonistic anarchy within their own lives, but the Stones stopped short of calling for the same across society.

The music begins in a driving, militaristic rhythm, as duelling acoustic guitars, a pounding tom-tom beat and some vaguely psychedelic undertones coalesce into a lo-fi mantra. With Brian Jones on sitar, and Dave Mason blowing a shehnai – a primitive Indian reed instrument – the sound swells into the kind of swirling pocket symphony the band had failed so miserably at on *Their Satanic Majesties Request*.

"WE NEVER REALLY FELT THE STONES WERE IN THE STREET, SO TO SPEAK... WE NEVER FELT THEY WERE PART OF THE STRUGGLE." **WAYNE KRAMER OF THE MC5**

The Rolling Stones may have been on the outside looking in on this sudden flare-up of youthful political rebellion, but the trip from Muddy Waters to 'Street Fighting Man' was less suspect than the distance between the Beatles' 'I Want To Hold Your Hand' and 'Revolution'. For front-line rock and roll agitators like the Motor City 5, 'Street Fighting Man' and the later, apocalyptic visions of 'Gimme Shelter' were at least a signal of acknowledgment for the movement. "We never really felt like the Stones were in the street, so to speak," MC5 guitarist Wayne Kramer says now. "It was nice they were sharing those sentiments, and they were great songs, but we never felt they were exactly part of the struggle."

Few sixties rock acts attacked the US political establishment with the same vehemence as the MC5 and the radical White Panther Party. Their manifesto promised "Rock and roll, dope, and fucking in the streets!" Thus the MC5 were the only band to show up outside the 1968 Democratic Convention in Chicago for a protest concert that was to have included the Jefferson Airplane, the Grateful Dead and Country Joe and the Fish. "They all chickened out," says Kramer. "When we said we were going to send the youth of America screaming down the streets, tearing down anything that would stop them from being free we meant it," Kramer says now, "although it was all in a certain amount of marijuana haze and uproarious laughter."

The Stones made rock and roll palatable to the bohemian aesthetic of bands like the MC5, bringing the rougher, challenging moods of blues back into the mix. While the early Beatles represented the good and clean side of sixties pop, the Stones were everything that was rude and surly about rock and roll. And the likes of 'Street Fighting Man' proved the Stones were brave enough to ask questions neither side wanted to hear. The song was banned from the Chicago airwaves during the convention.

"I'm not sure if it really has any resonance for the present day," Jagger said to Rolling Stone in 1995. "I don't really like it that much. I thought it was a very good thing at the time. There was all this violence going on."

STRAY CAT BLUES

As an exhibition of raw sexual appetites, 'Stray Cat Blues' lived up to every nightmare inspired by Andrew Oldham's slogan "Would you let your daughter marry a Rolling Stone?" The song's opening moments are all grunts and coos between Mick Jagger and some anonymous young woman, as Keith Richards amplifies the heavy breathing with a wickedly lean guitar lick. "I can see you're 15 years old," Jagger growls suggestively. "Bet your mama don't know you scream like that."

The menacing seducer is a recurring character in the blues tradition, preaching an insatiable lust without fear or apology. By now, the Rolling Stones had developed their own special brand of hedonism, exploring the limits of sex and drugs for all to see. The Stones were hardly unique in their reputation for devouring young groupies, but no band had dared transform it into a public celebration. This was at least partly role-playing, with Jagger tweaking a horrified establishment by living the life of Turner from his role in the film Performance.

The low rumbling of 'Stray Cat Blues' owes much to the Velvet Underground's example, songs such as 'Sister Ray' and 'Heroin' – all grim examinations of humanity spread across a canvas of stark rhythm and distortion. Richards puts his own blues-based spin on it, and Jagger welcomes yet another victim.

FACTORY GIRL

Beggars Banquet begins with an outrageous ode to the dirty work of Lucifer, but the scratchy country-blues textures across the rest of the album finally lead the Stones to a pair of songs on the working classes. In 1968, the lives of band members already shared little with the sad little people of these last two tracks, even if there is some affection between the lines of 'Factory Girl'.

Jagger seems to be singing adoringly of a woman he's waiting to emerge from her factory job – hardly one of the women of wealth and taste the Stones were now mingling with.

It's left to the picking and strumming of Keith Richards to bring some warmth and uplift to the song. If Jagger's feelings for the working women he had never met remain forever ambiguous, the organic acoustic sounds behind him at least seem able to tap into their world.

It's very possible that Richards knew nothing of any ironic twist in Jagger's lyrics during the recording of basic tracks for the song. "Quite often the words would get written afterward," George Chkiantz says of the Beggars Banquet sessions.

While Richards often played a part in crafting lyric ideas for songs, most of the details were left to Jagger. But the guitarist maintained some veto power if he didn't like something. "Mick is the one who does all the talking," says Chkiantz. "Keith will lay down on the sofa and listen, though he's obviously active and concerned. But Mick is very much the one who sits at the producer's desk and does things. But I very distinctly got the feeling that if Keith decided he didn't like it, that was the end of it. No arguments."

SALT OF THE EARTH

The final song on *Beggars Banquet* begins with a disarmingly simple sound: just the strumming of acoustic guitar, and the cracked vocals of Keith Richards. He's singing a song straight from the pub, raising his glass: "Let's drink to the hard-working people… the salt of the earth."

The track ultimately swells into an epic gospel number, with a choir and excited piano melody. But, once again, Jagger's response to the masses is ambivalence – "They don't look real to me, in fact they look so strange". But it's that first verse sung by Keith that makes it real.

'Salt Of The Earth' marked the first significant vocal appearance by the guitarist. "He didn't really know how to do vocals," says Chkiantz of Richard's big debut moment in front of the microphone. "He'd watched Mick do a million of them, but when it came to himself he seemed rather charmingly diffident."

DEMONSTRATIONS BY YOUNG PEOPLE WERE COMMONPLACE DURING THE SUMMER OF 1968.

Beggars Banquet remains among the very best rock albums ever recorded. And yet the Rolling Stones never considered themselves to be the voice of a generation – Jagger left such pronouncements to others. His passion was in the sexual danger of 'Stray Cat Blues' or in the eternal threat of 'Sympathy For The Devil'. With *Beggars Banquet*, basic elements of blues, rock, country and soul coalesced into the mature sound of the Stones. The days of pop and psychedelia were behind them. Everything the band would later become had its roots in *Beggars Banquet*. And with or without Brian Jones, they weren't ready to stop now.

LET IT BLEED

Recorded   November 1968 and February to November 1969,
Olympic Studios, London; Sunset Studios and Elektra
Studios, Los Angeles, California.

Produced by   Jimmy Miller.

Musicians   The Rolling Stones: Mick Jagger (vocals, harmonica),
Brian Jones (autoharp, percussion), Keith Richards
(guitars, bass guitar, vocals), Mick Taylor (electric
guitar, slide guitar), Charlie Watts (drums), Bill
Wyman (bass guitar), autoharp, vibes).
Additional musicians: Ian Stewart (piano), Nicky
Hopkins (piano, organ), Byron Berline (fiddle), Merry
Clayton (backing vocals), Ry Cooder (mandolin), Bobby
Keys (tenor saxophone), Jimmy Miller (percussion,
drums, tambourine), Leon Russell (piano), Al Kooper
(piano, French horn, organ), Nanette Workman
(backing vocals, Doris Troy (backing vocals), Madelaine
Bell (backing vocals), Rocky Dijon (percussion), The
London Bach Choir (vocals).

GIMME SHELTER
LOVE IN VAIN (JOHNSON)
COUNTRY HONK
LIVE WITH ME
LET IT BLEED
MIDNIGHT RAMBLER
YOU GOT THE SILVER
MONKEY MAN
YOU CAN'T ALWAYS GET WHAT YOU WANT

NEW KID IN TOWN:
PRODIGY MICK
TAYLOR *(SECOND
FROM LEFT)*
TAKES OVER LEAD
GUITAR DUTIES.

"THIS RECORD SHOULD BE PLAYED LOUD". Pay attention to these words, stamped on to the cover of *Let It Bleed* in great, bold letters. Read them not only as operating instructions, but as a warning. The Rolling Stones meant to assault your senses in 1969 – in ways both overt and wickedly subtle – with sounds that reflected the turmoil then rolling through the streets of America and Europe, and across the rice paddies of south-east Asia. It was a storm of sex, death and fear, where shelter and redemption seemed a distant dream.

For anyone who hadn't already noticed, *Let It Bleed* was here to proclaim the collapse of everything that had once seemed so sweet and innocent about the 1960s, a decade of utter extremes. Swinging London and San Francisco's Summer of Love were fading quickly. The muddy, good vibes of Woodstock still lay ahead, but so too did Altamont, which only added to the era's growing unpredictability. By now, both Robert Kennedy and Martin Luther King had been murdered. Men visited the moon that July, just as President Richard Nixon began a reign of dirty tricks, paranoia and ruthless calculation, with vague wartime promises of "peace with honour". Charlie Manson descended from the foothills of Los Angeles to lead a murder spree of the rich he hoped would unleash a race war, just as The Beatles' 'Helter Skelter' had somehow promised him. Another kind of insanity was sweeping China, where radical Red Guards continued a violent purge of the intelligentsia and all things foreign in Chairman Mao's Cultural Revolution. Russian tanks in Czechoslovakia. Bombs in Northern Ireland. Ted Kennedy at Chappaquiddick. Casualties everywhere.

Laying amidst the dead and wounded was Brian Jones. He did not live to see the December release of *Let It Bleed*. But Jones had long since ceased to be a creative factor within the Stones, the band that had once been his obsession, his creation. His masterplan of bringing the blues to the masses, to spread the word about the immortal Muddy Waters and Elmore James, had worked beyond his wildest fantasies – even if it also meant enduring the occasional Chuck Berry rocker at the insistence of Keith Richards. Yet fame and fortune hadn't been good for Jones. "He was very talented," Mick Jagger told *Rolling Stone* in 1995, "but he was a very paranoid personality and not at all suited to be in show business."

THE DEATH OF BRIAN JONES IN 1969 FURTHER ENHANCED THE PERCEPTION OF A BAND DANCING CLOSE TO THE EDGE.

That paranoia had come from repeated drug busts, his failing health, the loss of lovely Anita Pallenberg to Keith, and his obsession with being known as the leader of the Stones even after the band's creative energy shifted to the songwriting of Jagger and Richards. Meanwhile, his own talent slowly slipped away during a lifestyle of endless partying, lack of sleep and too much hanging out. Speed, morphine, cocaine, acid, booze. Even on *Beggars Banquet*, Jones' useful moments of inspiration had been few. But during the early *Let It Bleed* sessions, his appearances were sporadic and, ultimately, not welcome. At Olympic Studios a year earlier, Jones had asked Jagger, "What can I play?" The singer's reply: "Yeah, what can you play, Brian?".

When the Stones decided to tour in 1969, largely for financial reasons, it was obvious that Jones was not up to the task. He would have to be replaced. So Jagger, Richards and Watts went to Jones' new home at Hartfield, Sussex, outside London, to accept his resignation. On June 8, Jones officially announced his departure from the band: "I want to play my kind of music, which is no longer the Stones' music," Jones said. "The music Mick and Keith have been writing has progressed at a tangent as far as my own taste is concerned."

In reality, of course, he'd been kicked out of the Rolling Stones. Although this was – to say the least – an impossible act for Jones to follow, he was hardly suicidal. He had already started cleaning up his habits. And at his new country home, the former house of Winnie the Pooh author A.A. Milne, Jones made plans for a new band. He was soon talking with increasing excitement about his future with friends such as Alexis Korner and other members of the Stones. Then, on July 3, after a night of partying and swimming in his pool, he was dead. An unfortunate mixture of alcohol and barbiturates, combined with a hopelessly frail nature, led to his drowning. Richards sensed foul play at the time, but Jagger remains unconvinced. And the cause hardly mattered. Elmo Lewis was gone.

His replacement in the Rolling Stones was Mick Taylor, who emerged from the London blues virtuoso tradition that had already produced the likes of Eric Clapton, influenced by the stinging lead playing of B.B. King and Freddie King.

It wasn't Jagger or Richards who discovered the 20-year-old guitarist. Veteran British bluesman John Mayall had already encountered Taylor years before at a Bluesbreakers gig when the young musician offered to fill in for an absent Clapton. "He was only about 16 or 17, but we had nothing to lose," Mayall remembers. "We had two sets to play that night in some town hall somewhere, and he just joined us for the second set. He was astonishing. He knew all of our versions of the material. I guess he'd been down to the club many times and heard it. Very gifted young fellow."

Mayall lost touch with the blues prodigy, until he needed a new guitarist for the Bluesbreakers – both Clapton and Peter Green had since moved on. Taylor answered an advert in Melody Maker, and was quickly hired. "He has his own style, and is exceptionally good on slide guitar," says Mayall, who recorded four albums with Taylor.

Two years after Taylor joined the Bluesbreakers, Mayall disbanded the group to free himself to explore acoustic blues. Jagger was by then looking to replace Jones and called on Mayall, a man with a reputation for unearthing supernatural young musical talent. He recommended Taylor and the young guitarist was soon spotted at the Rolling Stones sessions. "He just jumped from one to another", says Mayall, who has periodically reunited with Mick Taylor over the years.

The full impact of Taylor's presence would not be felt until 1971's *Sticky Fingers* album, but the guitarist appeared at a crucial time for the Stones. There was the coming international tour, playing for a more sophisticated audience: no more little girls screaming through puberty, but massive arena crowds who actually expected to hear what the boys were playing.

Expectations for the Stones were bumped even higher with the single 'Honky Tonk Women', released the day after Jones' funeral. The song had been transformed during sessions from Richards' original country bumpkin concept into a brash, mid-tempo rocker through Taylor's influence. As 'Jumpin' Jack Flash' had done a year earlier, 'Honky Tonk Women' found the Stones pushing their straight-ahead rock and roll to an exciting new level.

The first look fans got of Mick Taylor came just days later at the previously scheduled free concert in London's Hyde Park on July 5. Accompanying the band on stage was a life-size cut-out of Jones, to whom the concert was now dedicated. Jagger read from Shelley's *Adonais* in Brian's memory, and released hundreds of white butterflies into the crowd. "We played pretty bad. Until the end, 'cause we hadn't played for years," Richards told *Rolling Stone* in 1971. "Nobody minded 'cause they just wanted to hear us play again. It was nice they were glad to see us 'cause we were glad to see them. Coming after Brian's death, it was like a thing we had to do."

Thus began a new era of live performance for the Rolling Stones. "It was the biggest fucking deal of the year", remembers Mick Farren, leader of the Deviants and a writer for *International Times*, London's first underground newspaper. He attended the concert with feminist writer Germaine Greer. "It was a whole fucking garden party backstage, and to penetrate that you had to go through lines of police, and then lines of Hells Angels. The British Hell's Angels were jovial, fairly friendly fellows."

Most recollections of the event neglect to include the scene brewing that same evening across the park at the Albert Hall, where the Who and Chuck Berry were performing. For some fans at Hyde Park, it was all part of the same full day of music. "There was a sort of rerun of the Mods and Rockers culture clash at the Albert Hall," Farren says. "All these Teddy Boys came out to see Chuck Berry and started throwing things at the Who. It was quite a spectacular evening."

The Rolling Stones were then in the midst of finishing *Let It Bleed*, a work destined to stand as one of the key albums of the 1960s. If *Beggars Banquet* was an explosive comeback after a season of muddled psychedelia, then *Let It Bleed* emerged as a more profound statement, a survey of the wreckage of an era.

The album cover bordered on the ridiculous, depicting a pop art five-layered cake – complete with bicycle tyre and movie film canister. It couldn't possibly represent the grim contents within. Lyrics were inspired by the months Mick was now spending in the US, along with constant reminders of the Vietnam War and campus uprisings.

Produced once again by Jimmy Miller, the Rolling Stones returned to their beloved blues, diving right into the source with Robert Johnson's 'Love In Vain'. Adjusting the arrangement to their own comfort, the Stones added extra chords and a deeper country flavour. On the album, and in published sheet music Jagger and Richards brazenly took full songwriting credit for the immortal blues tune.

Let It Bleed is also notable for Keith Richards' playing, which reached near-heroic proportions on the album. In the absence of Brian Jones, Richards' did most of the guitar work himself, layering both rhythm and lead work into passages of stirring nuance and gut-bucket drive.

The basic tracks for most of *Let It Bleed* were recorded at Olympic Studios in London, with final overdubs and mixing being completed in Los Angeles. The final album was an instant success, widening the boundaries of rock and roll possibility a little bit more. But back at Olympic, there was always some lingering frustration among the studio crew that some of the great moments they remembered would be wiped away by the time the album masters returned from the US. "If you work on a Stones album it takes about two years to come to terms with realizing it's going to be like that," says engineer George Chkiantz with a laugh. "At first it's like 'What on earth has he done to it now! How could he!'"

And yet, details aside, the final outcome could not be denied. If any work proved that what the Stones were doing was more than just rock and roll, it was *Let It Bleed*.

MERRY CLAYTON ADDED A CRUCIAL LAYER OF WARMTH AND POWER TO 'GIMME SHELTER'.

GIMME SHELTER

Welcome to the apocalypse according to Mick Jagger. And why not? The Rolling Stones were suitable messengers on the troubles shaking the populace. And fiction was hardly necessary at this point. No need to dance with Lucifer when napalm is already boiling earth and flesh in the name of freedom.

The West was still enjoying a post-war economic boom, but a crisis of conscience was emerging amidst a youth culture unhappy with the war in Vietnam and mainstream attitudes toward race, sex and free speech. Revolution was brewing, or so it seemed. And as rape, murder and war crept closer, Jagger's message was both a warning and a cry for escape. If war is "just a shot away", then so too is love but "a kiss away".

As Richards builds an ominous, shimmering backdrop of guitars, a haunted Jagger describes "the fire sweepin' our very street today". It's a story of the end of the world, as told through a song that critic Greil Marcus once declared as "the greatest rock and roll recording ever made".

The grim tremolo effect underneath Jagger's dreadful tale owes much to the Stones' endless search for interesting new sounds. "They discovered these Triumph amplifiers, tall stacks with an amp-top built in," says engineer George Chkiantz. "They were pretty terrible really. But Keith got into the fact that if you got these things just hot enough and on the way to breaking down, you suddenly got this sound out of them. They didn't use them a lot after that."

Singing alongside Jagger on 'Gimme Shelter' is Merry Clayton, emerging from Richards' distorted canvas with an angelic delivery of pure, haunted gospel. The veteran R&B backing vocalist had already appeared on records by Darlene Love and Ray Charles when she was summoned by the Stones. Her career would later lead her to some mildly successful solo albums and occasional acting parts, including a recurring role on TV's *Cagney And Lacey* in the eighties. Clayton's presence on the track added a crucial layer of warmth and power.

Producer Jimmy Miller used to tell a story of the Stones' first encounter with Miss Clayton, who was no wallflower at the Los Angeles vocal sessions. When she arrived at Elektra Studios, Clayton sauntered up to Jagger, looked him up and down, and said, "Man, I thought you was a man, but you nothing but a skinny little boy!".

Further discomfort came after Clayton had finished singing the first chorus of the song: Perfect! Amazing! Mick and Keith raved. It was then, Miller recalled to friends, that this woman with the lovely voice wanted to discuss royalties before moving on to that second verse.

COUNTRY HONK

To some ears, this country and western remake of the Stones' immortal 'Honky Tonk Women' was an act of sacrilege. But this is exactly how Keith intended it all along. If 'Country Honk' does not ring with the same kind of authenticity as the band's later forays into the white man's blues, the track at least reveals genuine affection for the genre.

It's been said that Gram Parsons used to spin George Jones discs for friends, and then mumble through his tears, "That's the king of broken hearts." No doubt, the Glimmer Twins were treated to a similar spectacle

KEITH RICHARDS LOVED COUNTRY MUSIC AND ITS CLASSIC STARS – SUCH AS THE LEGENDARY HANK WILLIAMS.

during their frequent trips to the US. It was Parsons who first brought Jagger and Richards into contact with real honky tonks. He shared his Merle Haggard and Jimmie Rodgers records, and sat at a piano patiently explaining the shades of difference between the sounds of Nashville and Bakersfield.

Richards' renewed interest in all things country emerges in a rich musical tapestry on 'Country Honk', which opens with sounds culled from the roadside: passing cars, car horns, tyres on gravel. He's soon strumming an acoustic guitar, joined by the tender fiddle-playing of Byron Berline. The song also marks the first appearance on a Stones album by Mick Taylor, who plays slide guitar. Vocals are more restrained than on 'Honky Tonk Women', and Jagger is joined by Richards and Nanette Workman (credited as "Nanette Newman") for a rousing chorus around a jug of moonshine.

"That's how the song was originally written, as a real Hank Williams/ Jimmie Rodgers/1930s country song," Richards told *Crawdaddy* magazine in 1975. "And it got turned around to this other thing by Mick Taylor, who got into a completely different feel, throwing it off the wall another way."

LIVE WITH ME

Here was a clue to the future. Listen closely and you'll hear the sound of the 1970s – of *Sticky Fingers* and *Exile On Main Street*. Here was everything that would epitomize the Rolling Stones, circa 1971: Jagger's nasty rap, the rollicking sax of Bobby Keys, Keith's relentless rhythm. 'Live With Me' was another prototype of a sound in the making.

The song glides along an aggressive bass-line played by Richards himself. But the key element is a the dual-guitar assault of Richards and Taylor – making the second of his two appearances on *Let It Bleed* – riffing toward some hypercharged rock and roll nirvana. Charlie Watts pounds a sinister rhythm, as keyboardists Nicky Hopkins and Leon Russell trade upbeat bar-room melodies.

Jagger meanwhile taunts a lover into woeful cohabitation: "I got nasty habits... Don't you think there's a place for you between the sheets?" Jagger sings of weird scenes and the promise of nightmarish domesticity, his flair for decadent humour – the ultimate manifestation of which would be 1978's *Some Girls* – growing ever sharper.

Saxman Keys makes his first appearance on a Stones track with 'Live With Me'. Here the band was at last incorporating horns as more than an afterthought, closer in spirit to soulman James Brown than ever before. Keys' ballsy honking would remain a central ingredient to the Stones sound both on record and on tour up through the 1980s.

Earlier in his career, to the never-ending amazement of Keith Richards, Keys had played with Buddy Holly. Keys finally recorded with the Stones in Los Angeles, but he was already a well-known commodity back in England. He and trumpet-player Jim Price were a couple of Texan boys who had arrived in the UK in 1969 as part of the illustrious 11-piece Delaney and Bonnie band. The duo quickly became in-demand session players in London, adding their horn chops to records by John Lennon, George Harrison, Ringo Starr, King Crimson, Mott The Hoople and Bad Company, although they wouldn't be credited together on a Stones album until *Sticky Fingers* in 1971. Keys and Price sold themselves as a team: Price wrote the charts, and Keys took the solos. "People would call us up, and we'd go over in the middle of the night," Price remembers. "They'd be stuck on something, and we would go and add a little colour that kind of solved the problem."

Between 1969 and 1974, Keys and Price recorded and toured regularly with the Stones, keeping pace in the fast lane. "Despite all this cowboy goddamn-them bravado bonhomie affect, underneath all that Bobby's got a mind as sharp as a fucking saber," says engineer Andy Johns, who worked with the Stones during those same years, and later would produce solo albums for both Price and Keys. "If you try and play chess with Bobby he always beats you in three or four moves. Every fucking time. Jim would come up with the parts, but his mind would drift, and often you'd see Bobby nudge him with his elbow to remind him to play something he'd written. So it was the cat's pyjama twins, man."

LET IT BLEED

Don't be fooled by the slight hint of deep blues suggested in Keith Richards' opening passage of bottleneck guitar on album's title track. Even when surrounded by an ocean of decadence, violence and drugs, there's virtually nothing within the grooves of 'Let It Bleed' to suggest any regret. Mick Jagger may be drowning in blood and decay, but it's merely some warmth and comfort – "a little coke and sympathy" – that he's really after, as he yelps across a stormy country tune from the Stones, including the

97

LET IT BLEED
SAW THE START
OF A LONG
COLLABORATION
BETWEEN SAX MAN
BOBBY KEYS AND
THE ROLLING STONES.

ever-reliable Ian Stewart on piano providing boogie-woogie in the service of blissful disintegration.

"They tended to lay the tracks down with Keith on acoustic," says engineer Chkiantz. "It's amazing how much of this type of rock stuff is actually founded on acoustic instruments. The acoustic or 12-string or harpsichord is very often welding the track together, even if you're not really that much aware of it."

Keith Richards surely understood the importance of that acoustic foundation, and worked hard at perfecting it. Chkiantz remembers one session when Richards took that commitment to the extreme, playing the same acoustic guitar chords endlessly in the vocal booth while Mick Jagger and Jimmy Miller argued about the most minute differences in the drum sound. When Chkiantz walked down from the control booth to adjust the microphones, Keith asked him what was going on. Chkiantz told him that his singer and producer were arguing about the drum sound. "Look, my hands are beginning to bleed," said Richards, who had been sitting quietly without complaint until that moment. "I've been playing the acoustic now for several hours. I won't be able to play it for much longer, and I really want to get this track down tonight. So you tell them to get their finger out of it."

The message was transmitted to Mick and the producer, who left the drums as they were. As Chkiantz passed through the vocal booth, he spotted Keith's guitar. "It was just covered with blood," says Chkiantz. "He must have been in considerable pain." Let it bleed, indeed.

MIDNIGHT RAMBLER

Dread is a recurring theme on *Let It Bleed*. It hovers over the album, exploding with terrifying assurance on 'Midnight Rambler'. During the 1969 tour, the Stones turned the song into a violent chant, drawing on fears attached to such twisted personalities as the Boston Strangler – aka serial murderer Albert DeSalvo. Jagger stood on stage, singing gravely of this nebulous force of darkness stalking your streets, your home, before whipping the floor in a frenzy. "Did you see me make my midnight call?"

Mick and Keith wrote the song while on holiday in Pasitano, nestled into the hills of Italy, a strangely pleasant setting for such a malevolent tale. They sat together in small cafes, Mick playing harmonica and Keith a guitar, cobbling together the chord changes, the tempo, the explosive horror story. "Why we should write such a dark song in this beautiful, sunny place, I really don't know," Jagger said in 1995.

There are scenes of greater violence elsewhere on *Let It Bleed*. For most of 'Midnight Rambler' the violence is implied, and therefore more weighted with impending doom. "Usually when you write, you just kick Mick off on something and let him fly on it," Richards said in 1971, "just let it roll out and listen to it and start to pick up on certain words that are coming through – it's built up on that."

Richards preferred the live version heard on *Get Yer Ya-Yas Out!*, which drew shattering force from the added guitar of Mick Taylor. The psychotic vibe of the tune emerged in the songwriting sessions. "It's just something that's there," Keith said. "Some kind of chemistry. Mick and I can really get it on together. It's one way to channel it out. I'd rather play it than shoot it out."

YOU GOT THE SILVER

'You Got The Silver' is the first song to be carried entirely by a Keith Richards vocal. It's a tender love ballad, no doubt inspired by Keith's new love affair with Anita Pallenberg. As ever, his raw vocals lack the richness and power typical of a Jagger performance, but there's something poignant and real about his delivery.

The track also marks one of the final appearances of Brian Jones, who plays autoharp here. He had by now burnt up his creative energies in an orgy of drug use, boozing and fear. Indeed, the person who arrived at Olympic

Studios occasionally in rock star finery was but a glamorous, empty husk of what was once Brian Jones. As far as the rest of the Stones were concerned, he really needn't have bothered coming at all.

"There were sessions where it was getting very, very ropey with Brian," says Chkiantz. So bad, in fact, that even when Brian gathered enough energy and interest to show up for a session, he often wasn't even plugged in by the band. "After that, things went slowly and then faster downhill. By *Let It Bleed* they were trying to keep him out of the sessions," Chkiantz adds. "And when he came it was just dreadful. The trouble is that you never knew if he was going to come up with a good one or not. It's true that at times nobody bothered to plug him in. But I don't think it was a consistent policy. It must have been pretty desperate for all of them."

BRIAN JONES WAS DEAD BY THE TIME *LET IT BLEED* HIT THE STREETS.

MONKEY MAN

Nicky Hopkins had many great moments playing piano for the Rolling Stones, inventing enough riveting passages to wonder aloud why he wasn't a full member of the band instead of a hired hand. That was perhaps a reasonable question, but one impossible to answer as long as Ian Stewart resided in the Stones universe. Even if they had been crass enough to fire poor Stu for image reasons, the band was forever grateful that he'd stuck around just the same. If Hopkins was destined to never enjoy his fair share of the rewards attached to the music he helped create, his playing was still a key element in some of the era's most important recordings.

Not that 'Monkey Man' stands as a particularly profound statement from the Stones, particularly in context with the rest of *Let It Bleed*. It's a showy, tuneful track, with a jumble of lyrics, making no particular statement, even if Jagger tosses in a "Satanic" reference. 'Monkey Man' is built on a very clever, up-tempo arrangement, mixing the elegant pop progressions of Hopkins with Keith's charged guitar riffs.

Hopkins had played with the Stones since the recording of *Between The Buttons* in 1967. "With his right hand he'd come up with these astounding melodic things, and his touch was perfect," remembers Andy Johns. "He never really screwed up. It was like a weapon you could use, really, on tracks. If you asked him to come in and dub something, it was like 'Oh, we'll use the Nicky Hopkins effect on this.' It was fantastic."

YOU CAN'T ALWAYS GET WHAT YOU WANT

The close of *Let It Bleed* remains one of the Stones' most famous epics, a sermon to the throngs of agitated youth awaiting guidance. To the streets? To the country? To Carnaby Street? Minister Jagger has your answer, or so he'd have you believe. And who wouldn't? The singer's voice is bolstered here by a massive singalong chorus, raising the stakes of 'You Can't Always Get What You Want' to Biblical proportions.

Yet it wasn't always this way. On The Rolling Stones' *Rock And Roll Circus* (finally unearthed in 1995 after decades in the vaults), the song is performed without the London Bach Choir. It's just the band stripped to its core, revealing a song with a quieter, darker message that touches on the desperation of the drug life and the unsettled times.

On *Let It Bleed*, Jagger begins the track singing against a backdrop of acoustic guitar, with a forlorn note blown on French horn by Al Kooper. Producer Jimmy Miller sits in on drums. By the time Jagger describes his meeting with the hipster junkie "Mr Jimmy", the singer is shouting above the beautiful racket of a gospel chorus and shards of electric guitar.

These are difficult subjects he's dealing with here, but for many listeners, the message of the song went no further than the title, a metaphor to the era's continuing disappointments, the falling short of one's youthful ideals – the song was used to melodramatic effect in *The Big Chill*. Appearing on the B-side to the massive 'Honky Tonk Women' single, 'You Can't Always Get What You Want' was widely heard.

Profound or not, the song put a close to an era. The Rolling Stones were heading into a new decade, where the Gothic flourish of a classical choir would never again seem necessary. They would instead crawl ever deeper into their own version of the blues, committed to an ever-hardening brand of riff-rock. With the Beatles about to implode, the Rolling Stones were well on their way to earning that ridiculous title: "The World's Greatest Rock And Roll Band".

STICKY FINGERS

Recorded	December 1969 to January 1971, Muscle Shoals, Alabama; Olympic Studios, London; Stargroves/ Rolling Stones Mobile, Newbury, Berkshire.
Produced by	Jimmy Miller.
Musicians	The Rolling Stones: Mick Jagger (vocals, guitars, percussion), Keith Richards (electric guitar, 6- and 12-string acoustic guitar, backing vocals), Mick Taylor (electric, acoustic, slide guitar), Charlie Watts (drums), Bill Wyman (bass guitar, electric piano). Additional musicians: Ry Cooder (slide guitar), Jim Dickinson (piano), Rocky Dijon (congas), Nicky Hopkins (piano), Bobby Keys (saxophone), Ronnie Lane (vocals), Jimmy Miller (percussion), Billy Nicholls (vocals), Jack Nitzsche (piano), Billy Preston (organ), Jim Price (trumpet, piano), Ian Stewart (piano), Pete Townshend (vocals).

BROWN SUGAR

SWAY

WILD HORSES

CAN'T YOU HEAR ME KNOCKING

YOU GOTTA MOVE (MCDOWELL)

BITCH

I GOT THE BLUES

SISTER MORPHINE

DEAD FLOWERS

MOONLIGHT MILE

ANDY WARHOL
DESIGNED THE
ALBUM SLEEVE FOR
STICKY FINGERS,
WHICH INCLUDED
A WORKING ZIP.

Behold Rolling Stones Records. Behold the mighty tongue, those bright red lips, and a sound both confident and fine, bringing rock and roll into a strange new era. The 1970s were finally upon us, and the snappy lips-and-tongue cartoon logo signalled that Jagger and his cohorts were now somehow "in charge". A ghastly development, no doubt, for the cops and tastemakers out to bring down these loud-mouthed London minstrels. Now they weren't even within reach – by 1971 the Stones had declared themselves tax exiles from Mother England, and were living in heathen splendor in the south of France, or wherever, and not much concerned about any bad news they might have left behind.

No longer would there be those irritating battles over taste and decorum. The first sign of a new enlightened age came in the form of *Sticky Fingers*, released by Rolling Stones Records, a "boutique" label distributed via a licensing agreement through Atlantic Records. Running the company was Marshall Chess, the 29-year-old son of Leonard Chess, the sainted founder of Chess Records. And for the label's first release, pop artist Andy Warhol created an audacious cover that depicted a suggestive pair of jeans, complete with bulging crotch and a working zip. Sticky fingers, indeed.

The Rolling Stones had been reborn yet again in the months leading up to the release of *Sticky Fingers*. Young Mick Taylor's impressive guitar was now fully incorporated into the band, and to great musical effect – evidence enough of this could already be heard on the single 'Honky Tonk Women'. And Mick Jagger was even threatening to become a movie star, with three films – *One Plus One*, *Ned Kelly* and *Performance* – all released in 1970. And the Stones were finally free agents, no longer indentured labourers for Decca Records in the UK, London Records in the US, or former hero and manager Allen Klein.

Equally important was the band's return as a touring unit. The sudden exit of the sadly dazed and confused Brian Jones now made it possible for the band to perform across Europe and the United States during 1969 and 1970. Powered by new sound technology, the Rolling Stones were now capable of filling sports venues with ear-rattling rock and roll. The screaming teenage girls were long gone, instead they had been replaced by enormous crowds ready to tap into the Stones' dark, bluesy groove. Outside the halls were the usual clashes between fans and police.

Then, of course, there was Woodstock, that massive rock festival happening in upstate New York that seemed to represent the hopeful side of sixties pop culture. Jimi Hendrix, the Who, Janis Joplin, Creedence Clearwater Revival, Crosby Stills Nash and Young, Santana, Melanie (!) and countless others had mixed with the rain, mud and acid for three days of mostly good vibes. All that was missing was a representative of one of the decade's great pop triumvirate: the Beatles, Dylan or the Stones.

At the end of 1969, the Rolling Stones sought to recreate Woodstock in their own image with a free concert in San Francisco's Golden Gate Park. After a experiencing a variety of problems with red tape, "Woodstock West" was moved to the Altamont Speedway in nearby Livermore, California. At the suggestion of the Grateful Dead, security was provided by the Hell's Angels motorcycle gang. It was here, in the days after the December release of *Let It Bleed*, that the Stones presided over an ignoble event that pop pundits would later declare the symbolic death knell for the era of peace and love – not that the Stones had ever fully identified with the hippie subculture, anyway.

Trouble began as the Hell's Angels rolled their motorcycles through the crowd toward the stage, solving security problems with pool cues and knives. Even Jefferson Airplane vocalist Marty Balin was beaten in mid-song for openly criticizing the Angels. And before the night was over, 18-year-old Meredith Hunter was stabbed to death while the Stones performed 'Under My Thumb'. Jagger was left to plead from the stage: "Who's fighting? What for? This could be the most beautiful evening…"

"WHEN CHARLIE WATTS GOT UP FROM THE DRUMS IT WAS A MASTER TAKE, AND THAT WAS IT. NOBODY DISCUSSED IT."

JIM DICKINSON, MUSCLE SHOALS SESSION PLAYER

Instead, it turned into the ultimate nightmare, witnessed by 300,000 fans, and captured by the documentary cameras of David and Albert Maysles and Charlotte Zwerin, whose footage would later be seen in the film *Gimme Shelter*. By the time the Rolling Stones made their escape via helicopter from Altamont, at least 850 concertgoers had been treated for LSD overdoses. Three others died as a result of various accidental causes. Already, the darkness was threatening to overtake them.

By the time the Rolling Stones arrived in Muscle Shoals, Alabama, for the first sessions of what would become *Sticky Fingers*, the disaster of Altamont was still a week away. Right now, they were a tightly wound rock and roll machine, riding the euphoric high of their first American tour since the demise of Brian Jones. As a result, the band experienced three impossibly productive days within the concrete tomb of Muscle Shoals Sound. It left them with the backing tracks for 'Brown Sugar', 'Wild Horses' and 'You Gotta Move', each song a career-defining anthem.

The Stones decamped at the nearby Sheffield Holiday Inn with little fanfare from the locals. Few in town seemed to recognize the celebrities in their midst, even with Keith Richards aswirl in scarves and snakeskin boots. Muscle Shoals session keyboardist Jim Dickinson remembers sitting at breakfast with the band when a waitress innocently asked: "Are you in a group?" "Yes," Bill Wyman replied, "We're Martha and the Vandellas."

The only limitation on the Stones was time – three days squeezed between the end of the official tour and the fabulous free love-in scheduled for San Francisco. So there was little of the meandering freedom the Stones enjoyed back in London.

The band entered the bare-bones studio (nestled within an old coffin factory) at the usual ungodly hour to begin working on 'You Gotta Move', a mournful examination of the soul by the North Mississippi blues immortal Fred McDowell. It was a song Jagger and Richards were already performing on the road as a duet. But what should have been a simple return to their roots was immediately bogged down in untested ideas, new arrangements, and Mick even attempting to improvise his own lyrics.

"I watched them for an hour, maybe a little more, and it just wasn't working," Dickinson says now. "I thought 'Well, here I am at a Stones recording session and I'm going to watch them blow it. This really sucks.' It really just wasn't working."

Dickinson left the studio briefly with writer Stanley Booth (who would later document his travels with the band in his book *Dancing With The Devil: The True Adventures Of The Rolling Stones*) to make a phone call and smoke a joint. When they returned, the studio was filled with the grim, languorous thumping of Charlie Watts, the electric piano of Wyman, and the forlorn scratching acoustic guitar. It was 'You Gotta Move', and it was working at last, with the dual moaning of Mick and Keith offering a shivering authenticity.

Three days in the Deep South could hardly transform the Rolling Stones into the real bluesmen they once admired as teenagers. And yet that first early morning session at Muscle Shoals demonstrated the ability of these five British players to tap into the raw essence of the real American folk blues like few others. "It's like they had turned into the Rolling Stones while we were gone," Dickinson says. "From that moment on everything they did worked."

BROWN SUGAR

The Rolling Stones hadn't come to Muscle Shoals on a whim. Not now, only days before the band's first American tour in four years was set to end with the free concert at Altamont. They had travelled to the Deep South in

MICK JAGGER AS THE AUSTRALIAN OUTLAW NEW KELLY.

search of cultural ambience, to tap into the kind of musical source material they discovered back at Chicago's Chess Studios, mingling with the likes of Muddy Waters. And yet this time the Stones would not be satisfied with a mere rehash of the ancient blues. Their recording of Fred McDowell's 'You Gotta Move' notwithstanding, the band's three days at Muscle Shoals were devoted to perfecting a sound that was undeniably their own.

The rich, edgy guitar that launches *Sticky Fingers* is the ultimate realization of what has been the band's signature sound ever since. The eclectic pop that had characterized such early work as 'Ruby Tuesday' now seemed forever behind them, replaced by a new darker wave. 'Brown Sugar' set an arch tone for *Sticky Fingers*, and rode a harsh groove borrowed from fifties rocker Freddy Cannon (best known for 'Tallahassee Lassie' and 'Palisades Park'). The song emerges from a blend of electric and acoustic guitar, some rude sax squealing from Bobby Keys – added later in London – and the nervous percussion of Jagger. 'Brown Sugar' moved like a supercharged locomotive, slicing through the Alabama air as rich as syrup. In short, it was straight ahead, state-of-the-art rock and roll.

Mick Jagger first sketched out the song during the filming of *Ned Kelly*, sitting alone in the Australian outback with an electric guitar to exercise an injured hand. By the time he reached Muscle Shoals, Jagger was slurring and mumbling words as confounding as 'Louie Louie', but leaving enough clues to suggest the man was singing happily about heroin, slavery and eating pussy. "God knows what I'm on about on that song," Jagger told *Rolling Stone* magazine in 1995. "It's such a mishmash. All the nasty subjects in one go."

The early morning sessions at Muscle Shoals benefited greatly from the band's tour, which had left them in fine playing form. "The way they did those songs, Jagger stayed on the floor with a hand-held microphone, walking around between musicians until he had all the lyrics nailed," remembers Jim Dickinson, who witnessed the entire three-day session. "And then he went in the control room with the engineer as the band played the rhythm track, at which point Keith took over the floor."

At one point, Dickinson remembers, a small problem emerged within the rhythm section. Charlie Watts' tom-tom was clashing harmonically with the bass, so it was suggested that he retune the drum. "No," Watts said casually, "I don't ever tune my drums." For a moment no one seemed concerned by this declaration, until Ian Stewart said, "Wait a minute, you can't just say blatantly 'I don't tune my drums.' That's a terrible thing to say." Watts remained unconvinced: "Why should I tune something I'm going to go out there and beat on? I'll just go out there and hit it and it will change."

The Stones would later re-record 'Brown Sugar' during a birthday party for both Richards and Keys, and were joined by Eric Clapton and Al Kooper at Olympic Studios. But not even that kind of firepower could capture the special ambiance of the band's three days at Muscle Shoals.

"Everything they did was at the peak of their competence," says Dickinson. "They reached the point where they did as well as they could do it, and that was their take. It was never discussed: 'Should we do this again? Is this a good take? Is this too slow? Is this too fast?' When Charlie Watts got up from the drums it was a master take, and that was it. Nobody talked about it."

SWAY

Jagger counts off a weary, lumbering beat at the beginning of 'Sway', before easing into the role of a man caught desperately adrift, his mind fragmenting from too many nights spent living "that evil life". A slow progression of twangy guitar chords suggest a dazed state of mind, as Jagger awakes to discover a new day that "destroyed your notion of circular time". He's still in search of some redemption when young Mick Taylor embarks a swelling blues lead that brings sudden and explosive clarity alongside the frantic piano runs of Nicky Hopkins and a subtle layer of strings.

For listeners still mourning the loss of Brian Jones, 'Sway' offered a graphic demonstration of the new musical possibilities his replacement brought to the Rolling Stones. In some ways, the result was truer to the band's initial blues fantasies than the endless pop experiments on sitar, dulcimer, and other exotic instruments, that Jones had pursued during the Swinging London years.

"After Mick Taylor came along, and they got a little bluesier – just straight-up blues rock and roll – it was fan-bloody-tastic," says Andy Johns, who witnessed many of the *Sticky Fingers* sessions as a sound engineer. "I used to like to watch the tracks come together, because they would literally write in the studio. So you would be able to see the whole procession of ideas that led to the finished song."

'Sway' also marked the beginning of another experiment for the Stones. It was the first track to be recorded at *Stargroves*, Jagger's Berkshire mansion. At the time of these first sessions in 1970, the typical mobile recording unit was a van packed with equipment that was then unloaded into a room, where the machines were held together unsteadily with string and gaffer tape. By then, however, the band had built the Rolling Stones' Mobile – a truck with the first self-contained portable recording unit, complete with control room. "I was petrified," remembers Johns, who was working on his first full album with the esteemed band his elder brother, Glyn, had engineered since the beginning of their career. "We're at Mick's house, I've never used this sort of gear before, and it's their new baby. So their expectations are pretty high. So I better dial it in or I'm up shit creek."

WIth the home studio in place, the band played together in a huge room at *Stargroves*. Johns had set up Taylor's amplifier in the fireplace –

KEITH RICHARDS
WITH ANITA
PALLENBERG AND
THEIR DAUGHTER,
DANDELION – SHE
CALLS HERSELF
ANGELA THESE DAYS.

with microphones placed up the chimney – and Charlie Watts' drum kit in a big bay window. The results for the tracks recorded there were spectacular. "It was fucking cool," says Johns of those *Sticky Fingers* sessions, "it really was."

WILD HORSES

'Wild Horses' began life as a lullaby. Keith Richards' first son, Marlon, had just been born, but the guitarist knew he would soon be leaving him behind for the crucial 1969 American tour. "It was a very delicate moment," Richards told *Rolling Stone* in 1971. "The kid's only two months old and you're goin' away."

The most significant element that transformed a simple love ballad into a wistful, epic exploration of devotion came when Mick Jagger rewrote most of Richards' original lyrics, keeping only the guitarist's signature line – "Wild horses couldn't drag me away". The inspiration would seem to have emerged from Jagger's own romantic life – he was still shaken from Marianne Faithfull's recent overdose-induced coma and their rapidly disintegrating relationship.

"Jagger was like a high-school kid about it," says Jim Dickinson, who observed as Jagger sketched out the final lyrics at Muscle Shoals. "He was crushed."

However, in 1993, Jagger claimed: "Everyone always says this was written about Marianne but I don't think it was; that was all well over by then."

'Wild Horses' was the final song the Stones would attempt in Alabama. But as the band prepared to begin recording, Ian Stewart calmly packed up to leave. Dickinson was then recruited. It wasn't until years later that Dickinson discovered the reason behind Stewart's disinterest in 'Wild Horses' – Stu had always hated minor chords. And the song begins with a minor chord. Even when playing live with the band on tour after tour, the committed boogie-woogie man would regularly engage in an act of perverse defiance, lifting his hands from the keys whenever a minor chord came up. "He was an extreme dude," says Dickinson. "He kept them honest. There was no bullshit when Ian was around."

For Dickinson, such as revelation was small compared to the spectacle of watching his beloved Rolling Stones up close in the studio. As he struggled to fit some appropriately tinkly Floyd Kramer country licks into the song, Dickinson realized the band was playing defiantly, if not obliviously, out of tune – a fact that demonstrated that in the world's greatest rock and roll band precision counted for little. As late as the mid-eighties, witnesses to their sessions would come away astonished at the rank amateurism of the Stones in the studio, where they were capable of showing little more expertise than the newest band of nobodies working on their worthless demo tapes.

But that recklessness was essential to the Stones process. And since Dickinson was unlikely to tell Richards how to tune up his guitar, he turned to an old beat-up tack piano in the back of the studio – where the band's roadie was storing the dope – and found an octave-and-a-half range he could play with one hand that was in tune with the Stones. It wasn't easy, but the immortal results of the final 'Wild Horses' track was ultimately a revelation to Dickinson, whose later career as a producer for the likes of the Replacements and the Texas Tornadoes has partly hinged on a certain looseness borrowed from the Rolling Stones, circa 1969.

"I've virtually based a career around what I learned in those three days," Dickinson says with a laugh. "It was so organic and natural, you just had to stop to think, 'Who's right and who's wrong here?' And they literally didn't have a clue as to what they were doing. They were making a record the way people off the street would come in and make a record."

And then, as the sun finally came up at the end of the band's third day in the studio, Jagger carefully packed up the final masters of their three new tracks before making absolutely certain that there was nothing left behind. "When the session was over, and they had the rough mixes, Jagger sat there and shredded the tape, except for the masters," observed Jim Dickinson. "He erased every mix and every outtake that they weren't taking with them. And he shredded the eight-track except for the masters, and ran the tape off on the floor. There ain't no bootlegs on that session."

CAN'T YOU HEAR ME KNOCKING

MICK JAGGER MADE HIS ACTING DEBUT IN THE CONTROVERSIAL *PERFORMANCE*.

The quick, grinding bursts of guitar that open 'Can't You Hear Me Knocking' are as minimalist as any punk riff that would emerge later that same decade. Never mind the Sex Pistols. This was a sound both brutal and wickedly real: the staccato riffing, the screech of fingers sliding across steel

strings, the distant yelp from Jagger – in fine ragged voice – taking the role of the Grim Reaper himself.

These are moments clearly dominated by the harsh rhythm playing of Keith Richards. From that tough-as-nails groove, the song soon drifts into the ether, shifting into an unexpectedly expansive second half that still has rock purists fuming. In the middle of this epic track – at over seven minutes, the album's longest – saxman Bobby Keys rolls into rich R&B runs and rude, jazzy honking as the Latin conga rhythms of percussionist Rocky Dijon guides the Stones into some rocking jazzbo that drifts perilously close to Santana territory. To some listeners, this was nothing more than pretentious junk. But 'Can't You Hear Me Knocking' was solidly within the rock and roll pantheon, not an exercise in aimless noodling. And *Sticky Fingers* was better for it.

If nothing else, the track further demonstrated the dramatic horizons suddenly open to the band via the slippery young fingers of Mick Taylor. The new guitarist introduced himself here as the kind of rock and blues virtuoso Brian Jones had once dreamed of becoming, before bad drugs and paranoia sent him speeding toward irrelevance, and a once-charmed life into sad oblivion. Of course, that's not to say that Taylor's presence changed the Stones fundamentally – after all, the overall sound of the *Sticky Fingers* era was established at least as far back as 'Jumpin' Jack Flash' in 1968. But Taylor did enable the band to expand on a purely musical level, and that was something both Jagger and Richards seemed to ready to explore.

"He had a big contribution," Jagger said of Taylor's playing to *Rolling Stone* magazine in 1995. "He made it very musical. He was a very fluent, melodic player, which we never had, and we don't have now. Neither Keith nor Ronnie plays that kind of style. It was very good for me working with him. I could sit down with Mick Taylor and he would play very fluid lines against my vocals. He was exciting, and he was very pretty, and it gave me something to follow, to bang off."

For Andy Johns, who mixed the Olympic Studios session engineered by his brother Glyn, witnessing the emergence of Taylor was a singular event in his career. Over the years, Johns would work in the studio with such guitar luminaries as Jeff Beck, Jimmy Page, Eric Clapton, Jimi Hendrix and on up to Eddie Van Halen. Yet even today, Taylor remains his favourite. "I could sit and listen to Mick Taylor all night," says Johns. "He would never make a mistake and every take would be different. And he'd make you cry. It really was good. He was a little bit hard to get in touch with as a person.

"HE WAS A VERY FLUENT, MELODIC PLAYER, WHICH WE NEVER HAD, AND WE DON'T HAVE NOW."
MICK JAGGER ON MICK TAYLOR

He was a very private man, didn't put out much. But I loved listening to him play night after night after night. It was not boring. Whereas working with Eric or Jeff or Pagey or even Hendrix you could get really bored. They're not on all the time, you know."

"I really think Mick Taylor had a big influence on the direction the band took. Who knows? After Brian left, and they started working with Jimmy Miller, and they did 'Jumpin' Jack Flash' and 'Street Fighting Man', obviously it got very much more rock and roll. Then Mick Taylor comes along and it really sort of put the icing on the cake. They went in that fantastic direction because they could start jamming again. They hadn't been jamming for a long time."

BITCH

Here was another explosive, archetypal Stones riff, another flash of rhythmic brilliance from the guitar of Keith Richards amidst the comforts of *Stargroves*. Yet the sessions for 'Bitch' actually began without Richards. By the time the guitarist arrived at the studio carrying a bowl of cornflakes, the Stones had struggled with the track for a full day without success. "It sounded bloody awful," remembers Andy Johns.

Richards calmly ate his breakfast as he watched the band at work, until he could stand no more of the terrible screeching: "Give me that fucking guitar!"

He quickly found a simple chord pattern that somehow transformed the song into a tight, agitated package. It was an absolutely relentless riff, a fiendish attack on the senses.

On the finished track, Richards' rhythm guitar is joined by the tenor saxophone and trumpet of Bobby Keys and Jim Price, along with some minimal lead guitar work at the edges. "Instantly it went from not very good, feels weird, to BAM! and there it is," says Johns of the moment Richards stepped into the studio. "Instantly changed gears, which impressed the shit out of me."

The sound the band had created was well suited for the lustful message from Jagger, as he grunted excitedly "When you call my name, I salivate like Pavlov's dog!" Further pushing the era's delicate boundaries of mainstream taste and decorum was the song's title – nearly two decades before gangsta rap and MTV welcomed the word into the common pop vocabulary – which was merely a more graphic expression of a theme that

had held Jagger's interest at least since the self-explanatory 'Stupid Girl' and 'Under My Thumb'.

UNCREDITED AT THE TIME, MARIANNE FAITHFULL WAS THE CO-COMPOSER OF 'SISTER MORPHINE'.

I GOT THE BLUES

Jagger doesn't even try to adopt some cartoon drawl here, and 'I Got The Blues' thus comes off less as another blues tribute than a deeper reflection of the singer himself. Too often in his work, Jagger has been strangely compelled to comically ape the vocal quirks and mannerisms of the original blues and country masters, as if he were still chasing those adolescent dreams of becoming a true bluesman. But as he sings this wrenching manifesto on heartache – presumably inspired by the end of his affair with Marianne Faithfull – Jagger glides sadly across the soulful gospel organ of Billy Preston and a soaring horn section arranged by Jim Price to an expressive style of lowdown blues that is undeniably his own – "I'll tear my hair out, just for you".

SISTER MORPHINE

The roots of 'Sister Morphine' stretch back to 1968, and a garden in Rome, where Jagger first began strumming this mournful tune. "It was a tune that Mick had that he didn't seem to have any words for," Marianne Faithfull says now. He played those acoustic guitar chords for months without lyrics before Faithfull offered her own, telling the bleak tale of a dying man crying out desperately for morphine. It was a story far from the delicate balladry of 'As Tears Go By', but it was also a chance for Faithfull to expand her repertoire to deeper, even dangerous material.

"I was envious of Mick and Keith," she wrote in her 1994 autobiography, Faithfull. "They had moved far beyond the boundaries I was still locked in… I had seen what the Stones were doing, what pop music could become. 'Sister Morphine' was an attempt to do that myself. To make art out of a pop song!" Other influences were in the air, including the Velvet Underground's 'Waiting For The Man', another junkie's tale.

Faithfull modelled her own song's structure after John Milton's *Lycidas*, and drew inspiration for the line "the clean white sheets stained red"

ONCE TOUTED AS A REPLACEMENT FOR BRIAN JONES, RY COODER PERFORMED ON THE HAUNTING 'SISTER MORPHINE'.

115

from an incident aboard a boat en route to Brazil where a pregnant Anita Pallenburg suddenly began bleeding. At the hospital, she was given a shot of morphine, much to the envy of her friends.

But at the time she collaborated with Jagger on the song, Faithfull had yet to fall into any serious drug problem of her own. For all the press about the "Naked Girl At Stones Party!" headlines, Faithfull was, like Jagger, still just a dabbler. For more than two decades, both have insisted the song is fictional, and not about Faithfull's subsequent experiences. "It was a story, literally a story, long before I ever took heroin or any other opiate," Faithfull says. "It was just a story that I had in my mind of a man who's in a car crash, and he's really in pain, dying in hospital, and he is the one asking for more morphine. It was really just an image. I wasn't really taking anything."

It was Jagger who arranged Faithfull's recording of 'Sister Morphine' during the mixing of *Let It Bleed*. On this recording, Ry Cooder plays accelerating bottleneck guitar like a man on edge, flailing across the rock-solid rhythm of Charlie Watts and Bill Wyman. The vocals were recorded in London. During the Los Angeles session, pianist Jack Nitzsche scolded Faithfull after he spotted the singer drinking booze and snorting cocaine. "How can you call yourself a singer and do coke?" Nitzsche demanded "Don't you know what that stuff is doing to your vocal chords and mucus membranes? Forget about Keith and Anita. Everyone in the band can get wrecked except the drummer and the singer."

Faithfull's first attempt to break free from her image as pop-chanteuse/rockstar's girlfriend was cruelly ended when Decca pulled her 'Sister Morphine' single from the shelves after just two weeks. By the time the Rolling Stones finally released the song on *Sticky Fingers*, laying Jagger's haunted vocals over the same backing track, Faithfull had begun her own struggle with hard drugs, including heroin. And the song would become what she calls her "Frankenstein", a dark creation that doggedly overshadowed her own life. By the end of the 1970s, Faithfull had beaten back those addictions enough to re-emerge as the wonderfully hard-bitten singer of *Broken English*, an album of stark intelligence and brutal experience. At the end of the 1990s she re-emerged as a refined interpreter of the Weimar catalogue of Kurt Weill and Bertold Brecht, and has since toured and recorded extensively. But the song is now left to the past.

"People can think what they want and take what they want, but I'm not going to promote morphine," Faithfull says with a laugh. "I'm not in the advice- and lecture-giving business, you know. These are big decisions that people have to make on their own. But I don't take morphine and I don't like it, and I don't see why anyone else needs to. That's probably a very old-fashioned view. But I don't stand in the way of people. They have to decide their own way of death."

Faithfull was left uncredited on *Sticky Fingers* for co-writing 'Sister Morphine'. The Jagger-Richards team received sole credit for more than two decades. Jagger now acknowledges that Faithfull wrote at least some of the lines, though he disputes the idea that she wrote all of the lyrics. "She's always complaining she doesn't get enough money from it," he said in 1995. "Now she says she should have got it all."

On the 1994 remastered version of *Sticky Fingers*, Faithfull was finally acknowledged as co-author of the song. "Isn't that wonderful?" Faithfull says. "Sweet of them!"

DEAD FLOWERS

If 'I Got The Blues' proved that Jagger didn't need phony accents to tap into the organic roots of American music, 'Dead Flowers' returned the singer to a style that was more play-acting than interpretation. Jagger later took that unfortunate inclination to the utter extreme with 1978's 'Far Away Eyes', which treats country music as a complete joke. This track is at least redeemed by a loose country groove, bouncing along a joyous boogie-woogie piano roll by Ian Stewart.

"I'll be in my basement with a needle and a spoon," Jagger sings happily, "and another girl to take my pain away". It's as if the singer has adopted the inherent optimism of country and western music to disguise some lingering sadness and other troubles.

"I love country music but I find it very hard to take seriously," Jagger told *Rolling Stone* magazine in 1995. "I also think a lot of country music is sung with the tongue in cheek, so I do it tongue in cheek. The harmonic thing is very different from the blues. It doesn't bend notes in the same way, so I suppose it's very English, really. Even though it's been very Americanized, it feels very close to me, to my roots, so to speak."

MOONLIGHT MILE

Sticky Fingers closes on an epic, wistful note. While Mick Taylor strums a rich musical canvas, Jagger sings wearily of being endlessly on the road "with a head full of snow," yearning to return to the bed of a loved one.

After a night of working on the track at *Stargroves*, with Taylor on guitar, and Jim Price plucking at the piano strings with a pedal down, 'Moonlight Mile' emerged in its final form at day-break. "We got it four or five in the morning, just as the sun was coming up," says Andy Johns. "It was dawn filtering through the windows, so it had that almost half-asleep feeling. It was gorgeous. I still listen to that song now and again."

Jagger would later recall 'Moonlight Mile', Taylor's restrained guitar and the lush string arrangement, with fondness. Richards had missed the session, but was equally upbeat about the result. "I wasn't there when they did it," he told *Rolling Stone* in 1971. "It was great to hear that because I was very out of it by the end of the album... We were all surprised at the way that album fell together."

EXILE ON MAIN STREET

Recorded	July 1971 to March 1972, Rolling Stones Mobile/Villa Nellcôte, Villefranche-sur-Mer, France; Sunset Studios, Los Angels, California, Olympic Studios, London; Rolling Stones Mobile/Stargroves, Newbury, Berkshire.
Produced by	Jimmy Miller.
Musicians	The Rolling Stones: Mick Jagger (vocals, harmonica, guitar, percussion), Keith Richards (guitar, bass guitar, backing vocals, piano), Mick Taylor (guitar, slide guitar, bass guitar, backing vocals), Charlie Watts (drums), Bill Wyman (bass guitar and upright bass). Additional musicians: Nicky Hopkins (piano), Bobby Keys (saxophone and percussion), Jimmy Miller (drums, percussion), Al Perkins (pedal steel guitar), Bill Plummer (upright bass), Billy Preston (piano, organ), Jim Price (trumpet, trombone, organ), Mac Rebennack (Dr. John) (piano, backing vocals), Ian Stewart (piano), Richard Washington (marimba), Venetta Fields, Shirley Goodman, Joe Green, Clydie King, Jerry Kirkland, Tami Lynn, Kathi McDonald, Lisa Fischer, Cindy Mizelle (backing vocals).

ROCKS OFF; RIP THIS JOINT; HIP SHAKE (MOORE); CASINO BOOGIE;
TUMBLING DICE; SWEET VIRGINIA; TORN AND FRAYED;
SWEET BLACK ANGEL; LOVING CUP; HAPPY;
TURD ON THE RUN; VENTILATOR BLUES; JUST WANNA SEE HIS FACE;
LET IT LOOSE; ALL DOWN THE LINE; STOP BREAKING DOWN;
SHINE A LIGHT; SOUL SURVIVOR

"I gave you diamonds/You give me disease". There's no escape from the real world of decay and desperation the Rolling Stones found themselves in by the early 1970s. These were lyrics scrawled right on to the cover art of *Exile On Main Street*, a musical document so fierce and chaotic that the Stones' early songs of sex and rebellion seemed almost wholesome by comparison.

Witness how far these London bad boys had come since the days of overgrown bowl haircuts. The Stones now seemed well beyond the reach of any recognizable authority, exiled to Keith Richards' villa in the south of France to wallow happily in a world of their own making, where middle-class values had gone terribly, terribly wrong.

This was no longer just rock and roll, but a rough, decadent sound with all hipster pretence stripped away. *Exile On Main Street* rolls through a mushroom cloud of urgent foreboding as grim as 'Gimme Shelter'. That its sense of danger hasn't dimmed over time owes much to a fanatical return to the rawest blues sound imaginable, finally transformed into a sound and fury that is undeniably theirs. As a package, *Exile...* is a mess of scattered images and sorrows, sending listeners on a travelogue of dysfunction and defiance.

MICK JAGGER AND NEW WIFE, BIANCA, MAKE AN EARLY PUBLIC APPEARANCE.

119

Reactions to *Exile...* in 1972 were heated and mixed. On first listen, the album's 18 tracks sounded like a catastrophe of sloppiness. Jagger was virtually unintelligible. That still didn't prevent it from topping both the British and American charts that year. But it wasn't until the seventies rolled onward that a critical consensus emerged, declaring the album a crucial pop document. Indeed, the remastered/extended CD package issued in 2010 arrived with such a fanfare that, almost 40 years after its original release, it went straight to the No. 1 spot in the UK album charts.

And yet the singer himself still needs convincing. "It's a bit overrated, to be honest," Jagger told *Rolling Stone* magazine in 1995. "It doesn't contain as many outstanding songs as the previous two records. I think the playing's quite good. It's got a raw quality, but I don't think all around it's as good."

That thumbnail analysis misses the album's larger effect. *Exile On Main Street* is not a collection of singles, but a bristling wall of sound. Jagger's judgment is undoubtedly clouded by the weird times that inspired the album's murky tales. His arrival at the sessions in the south of France followed his wedding to Bianca Rose Perez Moreno de Macias in St Tropez. It was also a time when tax problems, lawsuits and ex-managers still hounded the band. Keith had just survived a car crash, but was sinking deeper into various drug habits at Nellcôte, his rented palace in Villefranche-sur-Mer.

Although several tracks on *Exile...* were salvaged from earlier sessions at Olympic Studios and *Stargroves*, the essential core emerged during nearly six months of work in the south of France. Keith's villa overlooked a quiet fishing village on the coast of the Mediterranean. His rent was $10,000 a month.

"IT'S A BIT OVERRATED, TO BE HONEST." MICK JAGGER'S VERDICT

The Nellcôte sessions were relaxed but difficult. The electricity often failed, and it was so humid during the summer months that instruments repeatedly fell out of tune. Among the Stones cast and crew was Gram Parsons, who was AWOL from his duties leading the Flying Burrito Brothers to some promised country-rock nirvana. Although not credited, Parsons may well have sung backing vocals on 'Tumbling Dice'. He was certainly responsible for influencing Richards' increasing fascination with country music.

Final vocals were overdubbed later in Los Angeles, where the band's visitors included Neil Young, Joni Mitchell and Marc Bolan. What they witnessed was a band digging deeper into its roots, ignoring a growing trend toward the pretensions of classical music, where epic overkill from the likes of Emerson, Lake and Palmer rang laughably hollow.

The Stones would drift into their own bloated excesses soon enough, but *Exile On Main Street* captured them at a moment of charmed recklessness. It was there in the band's lecherous take on Slim Harpo's 'Hip Shake'. The Stones cut the track as raw Texas boogie, with duelling guitars, the clipped rattling of Charlie Watts, and Jagger moaning like a man caught in a trance. He falls deeper into Harpo's ancient spell during a harmonica wheeze that carries the low rumble of the sorriest of life's blues.

If *Exile...* is less memorable for its individual pop songs, the album's overall effect is profound, shaping a lasting monument to the most primal blends of rock and blues. "People say, 'Why the south of France?' It's just the closest place where we can relax a bit and then record," Richards told *Rolling Stone* magazine in early 1971, as the band prepared to begin work in his basement. "That's why we're all living in the same place... to transfer all that equipment. I hope it's worthwhile."

ROCKS OFF

Exile On Main Street starts off, fittingly enough, with a sharp progression of mid-tempo riffing, and a gravelly yowl from Mr Jagger. In these first few seconds, the tone for the album's 18 songs is indelibly set, and it's disarmingly relaxed.

There is a barely hidden fire that soon explodes with joyous abandon, cutting across a roaring riverbed of piano and horn. Jagger's voice is just another part of the mix, rarely demanding any more attention than the epic muddle of rock and blues going on around him. The dual-guitar assault, the tidy, vicious beat, Bill Wyman's thick, breezy basslines, all roll as one. It was if the "World's Greatest Rock And Roll Band" was just another juke joint jam session.

Thus the six months of recording on *Exile On Main Street* often depended on sudden bursts of inspiration. 'Rocks Off' was an early success at Villefranche-sur-Mer. Sessions for the basic track had gone extremely well, and by sunrise the next day even Keith had passed out. That was usually a signal to engineer Andy Johns to head off to bed himself. But once he arrived at the villa he shared with trumpet-player Jim Price a half-hour drive away, the telephone was ringing. It was Keith. "Where the fuck are you?" "Well, you were asleep," Johns replied. "I thought I'd go home seeing as it was five in the morning." Normally, Richards would have been inclined to wait for the next night's session. What was the hurry? But Keith was ready, supremely prepared for the delicate task at hand, and he wasn't about to let this moment pass. "Oh, man, I've got to do this guitar part," he said. "Come back!"

"So I get back, he plugs in his Telecaster, and he does the second rhythm guitar part, and the whole thing just came to light, and really started grooving," Johns remembers. Richards had the thing nailed in two takes.

The relentless riffing on 'Rocks Off' propels another tale of profound sexual frustration and impotence. Much that could be explicit is brilliantly slurred by Jagger, suggesting the steamy contents of a Henry Miller novel.

During the mixing of 'Rocks Off' months later, a strange echoing warble effect was added to Jagger's vocals, adding a dreamy layer to the bridge of this otherwise straight-ahead rock tune. "We got lucky on the sound of that," says Johns. "It's very cohesive."

The finished track also served to introduce horn-player Jim Price and saxman Bobby Keys as crucial figures throughout the album. The brassy sound from these Texan sidemen was big, brash, impudent and rude, much like the Rolling Stones themselves. Price acted as arranger for the horn section, and was delegated an unusual degree of autonomy. When the Stones were finished with the basic tracks, and left for a holiday in Montreaux, Price, Keys, keyboardist Nicky Hopkins, producer Jimmy Miller and Johns were left to handle the overdubs. "It was obvious which songs lent themselves to having horns," Price says now. "What was played was left up to us. They kind of liked what we did."

RIP THIS JOINT

This quick roadhouse rave-up is a blistering salute to the Stones' deepest rock and blues roots. Jagger's vocals are a frantic blur within a supercharged Chuck Berry groove, though even the old master himself never rocked this hard and fast. Look forward half a decade or more to the Clash and X for a suitable comparison.

The slashing Richards–Taylor guitar assault runs on pure adrenaline here, joined by the standup bass of Bill Plummer and a rollicking solo by Bobby Keys. 'Rip This Joint' was just one of the results from the all-night jam sessions the Stones led at the beginning of work on *Exile On Main Street*. "When we were in France we just jammed every night for two months," says Price. "We just played from about nine at night until about four in the morning. We'd just play, play and play. Then the songs would fall together. Mick started singing 'Mmmumngn-mmumbng' – nothing, just syllables, just mush. He would keep singing until words started to come out of it."

Price remembers that most tunes would begin with Richards working something out on guitar, in search of an appropriately snarling groove. "Sometimes Keith and Mick would write upstairs," says Price. "They would play and sing until something would take form."

CASINO BOOGIE

The slow shuffle of 'Casino Boogie' offers typically mush-mouthed vocals from Mick, making way for another energetic Bobby Keys solo. Richards plays bass. Some inspiration for both this track and 'Tumbling Dice' most likely emerged from the convenient proximity of casinos to these sessions in the south of France. Richards often spent his days at the craps and roulette tables near the villa shared by Johns and Price just outside Monte Carlo. It was a fine way to ease into the day, before crawling into the studio that night at Keith's house.

"Those albums weren't very difficult to make," Price says of his work on *Exile On Main Street* and *Sticky Fingers*. "It just took a long time, because it was very relaxed and kind of went on and on forever. But there wasn't any fighting or anything."

The raw, muddled sound heard throughout much of *Exile On Main Street*, Price says, "really comes from the instruments, because Keith would play with a certain kind of distortion on his rhythm guitar. That's just what it sounds like."

THE GUITAR WORK OF MICK TAYLOR HELPED RETURN THE STONES TO THEIR BLUES ROOTS.

TUMBLING DICE

Mick Jagger is the unlikely preacherman here, testifying to some great life lesson as the band eases into a throbbing groove. He's embraced by the warm gospel harmonies of Claudie King and Vanetta Fields as he flubs his words to great and frustrating effect, neither saying what he means nor meaning quite what he says, just as Fats Domino always said it should be.

Jagger also plays guitar here, while Mick Taylor handles bass. But the groove is all Richards. 'Tumbling Dice' glides along the album's richest musical arrangement, aligned with a steely Charlie Watts backbeat that brings some discipline to Jagger's sermon of defeat. Even a printed lyric sheet, free from Jagger's haunted soulman growl, leaves its message far from clear, but its loser's ambivalence is undeniable. "I don't think it's our best stuff," Jagger told *Rolling Stone* magazine in 1995. "I don't think it has good lyrics. But people seem to really like it, so good for them."

For many listeners, 'Tumbling Dice' ranks among the Stones' most memorable tracks.

But what sounds so natural and subtly hypnotic on record actually provided one of the most difficult recording and songwriting challenges during the making of the album. Originally entitled 'Good Time Women', with a completely different set of lyrics, the song stumbled through endless sessions of trial and error as Keith Richards struggled to finesse its central riff.

"With 'Tumbling Dice' we worked on that for a couple of weeks at least, just the basic track," remembers Andy Johns. "I know we had a hundred reels of tape on the basic track. That was a good song, but it was really like pulling teeth. It just went on and on."

The making of 'Tumbling Dice' was an extreme case, but it symbolized the atmosphere of lingering detachment that prevailed for much of the Stones' six months at Nellcôte. Drugs, lawsuits, sex, the decadence of isolation in the south of France, all the usual suspects were to blame. "We cared, but we didn't care as much as we had," Jagger said in 1995. "Not really concentrating on the creative process, and we had such money problems… We were really in a very bad way. So we had to move. And it destabilized us a bit. We flew off all edges."

However, the lasting power of *Exile On Main Street* emerged during those moments when inertia was suddenly overtaken by inspiration – when the Rolling Stones finally coalesced from the shambles into a band that really mattered.

"They were the worst bloody band on the planet, the worst bunch of musicians in the world… they could be for days at a time," Johns says with a laugh. "Really fucking horrible. And you sit there wondering how on earth are we going to get anything out this. They would play very badly, and that's how they played most of the time, very poorly, and out of tune. Most of it had to do with attitude. They did take a long time in those days, so Bill and Charlie were kind of waiting for the real spark to happen before everyone really bothered."

Watts and Wyman usually arrived at Nellcôte by 8pm. Richards typically made it downstairs to the studio by midnight, but was soon gone again – "Oh, hang on, I've got to put Marlon to bed." And he'd be absent for another hour or two.

"Trying to get all those guys in the room at the same time and actually really bother to nail something back then was very difficult," says Johns. "They were the worst band on the planet, BUT, when it happened, they were transformed almost instantly from this dreadful band into the Rolling Stones, and blow you away. It was almost magical."

SWEET VIRGINIA

The fabulous church of the Rolling Stones never rang with more crisp religious fervour than on this slow acoustic hootenanny. Waves of longing harmonica preside over 'Sweet Virginia', a track with all the spiritual force of a folk revival meeting on a backwoods porch.

"We can't play country music like authentic Chicago bluesmen," Jagger told *NME* in 1978. "We do our best, but we can't copy – that's not the idea. And so it comes out the way it does… different."

The track is a leftover from the Olympic Studios sessions for *Sticky Fingers*. Thus, the better separation between instruments, a marginal improvement over the muddle of Keith's basement. And yet the raw country blues of 'Sweet Virginia' fits easily within the thick sonic gumbo of the album. Ian Stewart scatters some piano runs deep in the mix, while the acoustic guitars do their delicate dance toward hipster transcendence.

Jagger isn't singing of salvation of the normal variety. His oeuvre remains that of the casual rock and roll outlaw, blending sex, drugs and rebellion to uncertain ends. He sings here of "tryin' to stop the waves behind your eyeballs", while cataloguing a fistful of reds, greens and blues from his local street pharmacist. "And I hid the speed inside my shoe." Lord have mercy.

GRAM PARSONS WAS AN IMPORTANT PRESENCE ON THE RECORDING OF *EXILE ON MAIN STREET*.

TORN AND FRAYED

Hard truths emerged from Keith Richards' basement. The Stones eased into the long, wearying *Exile On Main Street* sessions never quite knowing if what they were creating was a wonderful, profound mess, or simply a tragic waste of tape and talent. "I don't think it was particularly pleasant," Jagger told *Rolling Stone* magazine's Jann Wenner in 1995. "I didn't have a very good time."

The great irony of *Exile On Main Street* is that while the Stones were en route to one of their greatest creative triumphs, maestro Richards was falling deeper into drug dependency. And booze and drugs certainly flowed freely at their Mediterranean hideaway. These were habits Richards wouldn't be able shake until his monumental 1977 drug bust in Toronto, when it became terribly clear that his addictions not only threatened his own health and freedom, but the future of his beloved Stones. And yet the guitarist performed brilliantly throughout the album, leading the band to a vast timeless sound, a defiantly organic mixture of blues, folk, country and rock, all marked by a troubled fraying at the edges. The recordings had a tendency to drift off course within the regular unstructured scenes at Keith's villa.

Jagger remembered the sessions later as "Just winging it. Staying up all night… It was this communal thing where you don't know whether you're recording or living or having dinner; you don't know when you're going to play, when you're gonna sing – very difficult. Too many hangers on. I went with the flow and the album got made. These things have a certain energy, and there's a certain flow to it, and it got impossible. Everyone was so out of it."

The implications of that life were brought into sharp focus on 'Torn And Frayed'. Jagger rides a breezy country groove here and sings of a rock and roll desperado, trapped on the uncertain edges of a world of the Stones' own making. It's a rock fable that's all too real. Did Richards recognize himself in the character of Joe the guitar player? Jagger sketches Joe as a figure of profound restlessness, lost in a haze of stardom and decadence.

The presence of Gram Parsons at Nellcôte is likely to have provided a jolt of Bakersfield-Nashville country and western inspiration on 'Torn And Frayed'. Al Perkins adds some springy steel guitar, as Jagger sings in a countrified drawl of ballrooms, smelly bordellos and parasite-filled dressing rooms. The lyrics could as easily have been about Parsons as his pal Richards. Both shared a rootless and reckless existence, and both found themselves within a lingering crowd of dubious hangers on. Parsons became a casualty of that world in September 1973, when he died in the California desert idyll of Joshua Tree from a probable drug overdose.

"There were a lot of funny people always drifting in and out," says Andy Johns recalling the sessions for *Exile On Main Street*. "When I showed up, there were a lot of people still there from when Mick got married, which was months earlier, just leeching off of Keith, and various dope dealers who would arrive and disappear. Keith used to have a lot of fucking wankers hanging around, let's be honest. The fucking dregs, but they were all getting him high. And Mick had his posh friends hanging around, but they really wouldn't come to the sessions that much. Some very disastrous people."

The final recording of 'Torn And Frayed' also marked a rare appearance on organ by trumpet-player Jim Price. It was typical of the often accidental nature of the Stones' creative process. During sessions for the song, listening to the band, Price was inspired to tap at a nearby Hammond organ. He didn't realize that he could be heard in the control room, and that Johns and Miller would decide to record it.

"There were a lot of rooms and all the different instruments were set up in separate rooms," says Price. "I went into that room, picked up the headphones and started listening, and just started playing the organ. It was just for fun. They did a bunch of takes on it, and I never knew that they had used it until I saw it on the record." Log another triumph for reckless abandon.

SWEET BLACK ANGEL

'Sweet Black Angel' was another leftover from *Sticky Fingers*, this time from the sessions at *Stargroves*, Jagger's manor in Berkshire. The working title – 'Bent Green Needles' – had been Keith's idea of a joke. It was recorded in a similar casual style as the Nellcôte sessions, with two acoustic guitars, Jimmy Miller on percussion, and everything bleeding into one another's microphones.

127

"That was done all of them in a room in a circle at the same time, because there was this one room away from the main hall that had no furniture in it, with a wooden floor, quite high ceilings and plaster walls," says Andy Johns. "We wanted to get the sound of the room." The result was a crisp hillbilly shuffle, upbeat and funky, with marimbas to add a vaguely Caribbean feel. Across that rich acoustic fabric, Jagger penned an example of extreme black caricature to rival Uncle Tom's Cabin. Finding the appropriate sharecropper's twang, he sang of "Ten little nigga, sittin' on de wall… free de sweet black slave!" Of course, Jagger's foray into bonehead quasi-Ebonics was meant as great irony, an unusual gesture of political support for the black American radical Angela Davis. The singer had previously shown little patience for specific political movements even as the Stones documented a darkening mood in the late-sixties via 'Street Fighting Man' and the apocalyptic 'Gimme Shelter'. And yet Jagger found something compelling about the dramatic image of Davis, whose hair was grown into a tall "afro" – a symbol of cultural pride in the era of the Black Power movement. "She's a sweet black angel," Jagger sang, "not a gun-totin' teacher, not a red-lovin' school mom."

Davis was openly communist and aligned herself with the Black Panthers when outraged California Governor Ronald Reagan targeted her for removal as a teacher at UCLA. She went into hiding in 1970 and landed on the FBI's "10 Most Wanted" list after being accused of aiding an attempted courtroom escape in Marin County that ended with four people dead. By the time of the album's release in June 1972, Davis had been captured at a motel in Manhattan and was awaiting trial. She was ultimately acquitted by a jury after a high-profile court battle that struggled with issues of class and race.

Along the way, Davis called for the overthrow of the US government and declared in her 1974 autobiography, "Jails and prisons are designed to break human beings, to convert the population into specimens in a zoo – obedient to our keepers, but dangerous to each other." That's tough talk for a jet-setting rock star to be embracing, though Jagger was likely more attracted to Davis as compelling feminine symbol – more smitten than engaged. It's doubtful, too, that Davis would have appreciated Jagger's other tribute to African-American women – 1978's 'Some Girls', which suggested that "black girls just want to fuck all night…"

Davis would become the vice-presidential candidate of the US Communist party in 1980, and spend the Reagan–Thatcher era drifting into middle age. She travelled the world in support of civil disobedience, racial parity, the feminist and peace movements and the fight against apartheid in South Africa. Jagger, meanwhile, was occasionally spotted at the British House of Lords watching longingly from the gallery.

"Rock and roll isn't protest, and never was," Jagger told *Rolling Stone* in 1980. "It's NOT political… It promotes inter-familial tension. It USED to. Now it can't even do that, because fathers don't ever get outraged with the music… So rock and roll's GONE. It's all gone."

LOVING CUP

Amidst all the tracks of grim foreboding on *Exile On Main Street*, the Rolling Stones find a hopeful vibe on this passionate estimation of the gospel sound. 'Loving Cup' was first heard in rough form at the Hyde Park concert in 1969.

By the time of this recording, Mick Jagger had clearly decided the song could do without any attempts at the exotic lingo of the Deep South. Instead, his delivery is natural and direct, and thus a more authentic reflection of the ancient musical influences that inspired him.

THE *EXILE ON MAIN STREET* SESSIONS SAW KEITH RICHARDS' DRUG PROBLEMS SPIRALLING OUT OF CONTROL.

The track plays out against the bouncy piano uplift of Nicky Hopkins, as Jagger portrays the usual down-on-his-luck hustler, looking for some spiritual redemption in small favours. "Yes, I'm fumblin', and I know my car don't start," he sings. "Just one drink from your loving cup?"

Tough riffing and a sharp backbeat soon emerge in the mix, but retreat in time for a deep wheeze from the horns of Keys and Price, who probably played this brand of American soul for real back home.

HAPPY

Keith Richards had clearly been a key creative force in virtually everything written and recorded by the Rolling Stones. He was no god-like lead guitar hero in the mould of Eric Clapton or Jimmy Page. But this was the man who had DREAMT the central riff and key phrase to '(Can't Get No) Satisfaction', no less. And during a relentless decade of work, Richards had refined the underappreciated fine art of rhythm guitar to spectacular new ends. Yet it is the casual, euphoric mess of 'Happy' that is so often seen as the Richards signature tune – the guitarist's special moment behind the mike on most of the band's subsequent tours. For fans, 'Happy' captured the reckless joy at Keith's core.

There is the usual rhythm pattern charged with attitude and drive. Richards' vocals are more ragged and thin on 'Happy' than on some of his other performances, but the spirit captured here is hard to resist, further uplifted with well-positioned harmonies from Jagger. "That was a lot of fun," says Andy Johns of the session. "It made us happy."

The initial session in France for 'Happy' was casual even by *Exile On Main Street*'s standards: Richards sang, and played guitar and bass; on drums was Jimmy Miller, while Bobby Keys added some percussion. The horns were overdubbed later, says Johns, "and it really came to life."

The recording of 'Happy' was so effective that there was soon talk of a Keith Richards solo album. Not that Keith was interested in the idea. Further evidence of the possibilities of such a project emerged at the most casual of moments. Johns remembers some of those moments coming during the elaborate lunches the band and crew often shared at Richards' villa, where a French chef was hired to keep the rock and roll commune sated on the delicacies of his stuffed tomatoes, sautéed asparagus and other fine foods. "This guy would make this luncheon deal on a big table out on the terrace, gorgeous to look at, let alone eat," says Johns. "This guy was a genius, a real artist. You'd sit on this big terrace and look out on the Mediterranean, and all these big yachts. Then Keith would come down and go 'I wanna cheeseburger.' After these great lunches Keith would sit down on these steps that went down to the garden, and just bang around on his guitar and sing. He was just wonderful on his own."

Johns was among those who repeatedly told Richards he should make a record of his own. But Keith's response was always the same: "Well, if I did that I would just want to use the guys in the band, so it would be a Stones album. So what's the point?"

Over the next few years, Richards gradually began to entertain the idea. At one point, Richards and Johns even had a meeting to discuss a solo project, which would include some heavyweight sidemen that Johns had already approached. "We had talked about it on the phone several times," says Johns. "We were going to do this, it was going to happen." But their big meeting was inconclusive. "He had been up for three or four days, and was passed out. He only woke up for five minutes... And then he went back to sleep."

"I KEPT PUTTING OFF MAKING A SOLO ALBUM FOR A LONG TIME, BECAUSE MAKING IT WOULD MEAN THAT I HAD TO ADMIT TO MYSELF THAT I FAILED TO KEEP MY BAND TOGETHER."
KEITH RICHARDS

They met again in New York in 1976. "Yes, you're right, we're going to do this!" said Keith. Then nothing, until 1978, when Richards released a single of Chuck Berry's 'Run Run Rudolph' and Jimmy Cliff's 'The Harder They Fall' as a lark. This was right in the midst of the Stones' rebirth as a band via the acclaimed *Some Girls* album, so he was in no mood to strike out on his own. Not yet. Richards' debut as a solo artist wouldn't come until 1988, but by then the Stones' future seemed very much in doubt. Mick had forced the issue by releasing two solo albums of his own during a growing estrangement with Richards. Although his *Talk Is Cheap* was critically acclaimed (unlike the Jagger LPs), Keith was not a happy man in 1988. "I kept putting off making a solo album for a long time, because making it would mean that I had to admit to myself that I failed to keep my band together," Richards told the *Chicago Tribune* that year. "How am I going to play, without Charlie Watts to give me the beat?" It was a scenario unthinkable back in those days of decadence in the South of France.

TURD ON THE RUN

The blood-hot hoodoo of 'Turd On the Run' features some of Jagger's most driving, hypnotic harp-playing. He sets in motion a twangy North Mississippi trance rhythm here in the tradition of the late blues immortal Fred McDowell – the composer of 'You Gotta Move', covered on *Sticky Fingers* – whose fine example taught a young Mick Jagger the crucial rules of sex and sorrow.

As Richards and Taylor send tears and fireballs from their guitars, Jagger plays and moans ominously, spitting out his lyrics on tortured love like a hyperactive hillbilly. Love, sex, diamonds, disease. The man's on his knees and crying – "I've lost a lot of love over you!" He's Mr Bad News on 'Turd On the Run,' rushing through these straight-ahead madman blues with raw, primal force. It's an utterly authentic recasting of the folk blues in the Stones' own image, played like some euphoric, mesmerizing revelation on the neglected roots of pop music.

During his wheezing moments blowing harmonica passages alongside Richards' acoustic chicken scratching, Jagger was at his most musically pure. "He's not thinking when he's playing harp," Keith told Lisa Robinson in 1989. "It comes from inside him. He always played like that, from the early days on."

VENTILATOR BLUES

It wasn't just lingering vibes from the old blues immortals that were capable of casting a dark spell over the *Exile On Main Street* sessions. And Robert Johnson wasn't the only man ever said to have sold his soul to the devil. If the Stones were in search of inspiration regarding the dark side of the human soul, they need not have looked any further than Keith's fabulous Villa Nellcôte, set on the edge of the French Riviera at Villefranche-sur-Mer. Built in the late 1890s by a financier named Eugene Thomas, ownership of Nellcôte had passed to the Bordes family, whose fortune had come from shipping soda nitrate between Chile and France. However, the building had been seized as a local Gestapo headquarters during the Nazi occupation of Vichy France during World War II, and visitors would notice how the floor vents to the basement were in the shape of Swastikas. "I imagine that downstairs in the basement, where things were always peculiar – we had fires – is where they would interrogate prisoners," Johns told journalist Craig Rosen in 1994. "So God knows what sort of behaviour was going on down there."

On this track Taylor earns his first and only co-writing credit on a Stones album. Jagger sings 'Don't fight it!" forcefully. According to Johns, the song was inspired by the real-life conditions there. Just one small window served the room where most of the band was set up, with a tiny electric fan spinning above Watts. Ventilation was at a minimum. "It would get very steamy down there," Johns says of that summer in the Mediterranean, "so we would have the ventilator blues."

JUST WANNA SEE HIS FACE

This thumper was another of the album's accidental ingredients. It began as a lo-fi recording of Jagger sitting in a chair singing while Keith played keyboards, and its deep echoes sound as if they were captured in some cavernous old cathedral. 'Just Wanna See His Face' was initially taped for reference, but the recording captured a haunting, soul-searching vibe that was worth preserving. Miller's percussion comes on like distant thunder. Both Taylor and Bill Plummer play low, rumbling bass-lines. And Jagger is practically scat singing here, moaning and grunting and mumbling about Jesus. The ghostly backing vocals were added later.

JUMPING JACK FLASH - MICK JAGGER CAPTURED IN FULL FLIGHT.

LET IT LOOSE

There's no mistaking that voice on the other end of the line. Singer Tammi Lynn had heard it many, many times – the vaguely irritated New Orleans growl, rasping like Louie Armstrong with a migraine. "Hey, Tammi," her caller croaked into the phone. "Hey, man! Check this out... fuckin' session cat called me, said be at the session, gonna be a session and shit, I don't know who it is, let's meet down there."

This was, of course, Mr Mac Rebennack calling, otherwise known as Dr John Creaux, the Night Tripper, master of the voodoo blues, who had often called on young Tammi to sing on his own records. Both shared a musical background rooted in the sounds of New Orleans, the same festering gumbo that spawned the Meters, Allen Toussaint and Professor Longhair. Although Dr John's only Top Ten American hit single – 'Right Place Wrong Time' – would not come until the following year, the singer-keyboardist had already been an established solo act since 1968. And when he travelled to England in 1971 to record his album The Sun, Moon & Herbs, he was joined by the likes of guests Mick Jagger and Eric Clapton.

Now Dr John was summoning Tammi Lynn down to Sunset Sound studios in Hollywood for another session. "He didn't tell me it was the Stones," Lynn says now. Not that it would have fazed her. She began her career as a jazz singer, bouncing from be-bop to Creole funk, and over subsequent years would appear on records by Wilson Pickett and Bob Dylan, among many others. When Lynn arrived at the session, she found not only the Rolling Stones in charge, but discovered she was to be part of a vocal group that also included veteran New Orleans R&B singer Shirley Goodman. During the 1950s, Goodman launched her career with Shirley & Lee, and enjoyed the hits 'Feel So Good' and 'Let The Good Times Roll'. (In the mid-seventies, Shirley & Company tapped into the disco craze with the breathy New Orleans funk of 'Shame, Shame, Shame'.)

Together, Lynn, Goodman and Dr John were among a half-dozen singers harmonizing until dawn. Lynn remembers working on four songs that night, though the singers are credited on *Exile On Main Street* only for the regretful gospel track 'Let It Loose'. Bathed under a soothing blast of horns, the gospel harmonies join the desperately pleading vocals of Jagger.

The basic track had been recorded at Olympic Studios in London months earlier, with the backing vocals added later at Sunset. "There was one particular line in something that was really raunchy," says Lynn of her night with the Stones. "It was a really, really raunchy line. I thought, We're out there, this is kind of good. This is like breaking all the rules." There was much common ground in the room that night between these singers, each of them exiles from London or New Orleans, which became obvious from Jagger's instructions to his makeshift choir. "What he wanted was this funk feeling, this real honest church feel. He had an appreciation for black music, and he said it openly," says Lynn, "so that was out of the way. We knew he had this affinity for the blues and where it came from. Wilson Pickett came clearly out of a church, out of a black experience. Mick came out of a respect for black experience, or black music. The greatness comes out of the spirit."

Years later, Dr John would grumble bitterly about the lack of credit the Stones had given to the richly talented players and singers he'd brought to the Los Angeles sessions. On 'Sweet Black Angel', the marimbas are mysteriously credited to "Amyl Nitrate", which Dr John insists should have gone to percussionist Richard Washington.

Lynn remembers the all-night session more fondly, describing it a quarter-century later as "very loose, very creative, very artistic." She adds, "When you're making music you don't know you're making history. You go in to have fun, you hang out all night and you party."

Her lasting impression of Richards is that of a quietly open player, absolutely honest and even humble, the furthest thing from a superstar. She'd had no contact with the Rolling Stones since then, other than bumping into Jagger years later at a Hollywood restaurant. But when the *Voodoo Lounge* tour passed through Los Angeles in 1994, Lynn left her front row seat at the Coliseum, and strolled up to the side gate. "I'd like to speak to Mick," she told the security guard, realizing she probably sounded like any other groupie crowded near the stage. Mentioning that she had appeared on *Exile On Main Street*, word got backstage to Richards, who had her sent to his dressing room. She noted that little had changed. "Keith just seems real human. He's a musician and he knows he's had a life that has had good and bad in it, and it's made him a better person for it."

After the concert, Richards sat amidst an ocean of food with friends and family. "It was very relaxed, laughing and talking about yesterday. He felt good."

ALL DOWN THE LINE

All that tape. All those months in France. Certainly the Rolling Stones had achieved SOMETHING. But just what? This was the question Jagger and Richards had begun to ask themselves when they arrived in Los Angeles to finish vocals and other bits and pieces for *Exile On Main Street*. No doubt, their new pals at Atlantic Records were asking much the same thing. The Glimmer Twins had long grown accustomed to working at their own pace, burning up time and tape like cigarettes as the band pounded away at some riff or bridge in search of that transcendent moment. In France, the only schedule that mattered was their own. And yet that internal pressure to put out a new single, to get back on the air, to maintain their presence in the ever-churning flow of pop culture hadn't faded from the early days.

So 'All Down the Line' was chosen, not because it was the track best suited for pop radio, but because it was the song closest to completion. Certainly, the song offered a driving rock sound, built on the charged chords of Richards, along with brief flashes of lead from Taylor. The elegant, blissful horns of Bobby Keys and Jim Price mingle with a chorus of urgent backing vocals as Jagger inquires, "Won't you be my little baby for a while?" Soulful and rocking.

That musical balance was still a distant goal when Andy Johns was summoned to mix down the track in Los Angeles. The individual elements were ready when Johns and the band began work on the final mix, but it just wasn't coming together. After hours of ear-numbing work, Johns felt he was losing perspective. He muttered, "Too bad I can't hear this on the radio." Jagger replied, "Oh, we can do that." The singer handed Stu a copy of the tape, with directions to deliver it immediately to a local radio station. In late 1971, any Los Angeles rock broadcaster would have been ecstatic at the opportunity to preview a new Stones single for its audience, even in the middle of the night. So at about 2am, Jagger, Richards, Watts and Johns climbed into a limousine for an early morning moonlight drive. "Next thing I know, I'm going up and down Sunset Boulevard, and one of the stations is playing it over the air so we can listen in the car," Johns says. "I still couldn't tell. It was a bit too surreal."

STOP BREAKING DOWN

If *Exile On Main Street* did not present Mick Taylor with the kind of showcase for epic lead playing that certain tracks on Sticky Fingers had, the double album's deep rock and blues canvas at least inspired some memorable flashes from the youngest Stone. 'Stop Breaking Down' was a leftover track from Olympic Studios that had captured Taylor's dynamic slide-guitar work.

"I learned a lot from Mick Taylor because he is such a beautiful musician," Richards told *Guitar Player* magazine in 1977. "I mean, when he was with us, it was a time when there was probably more distinction, let's say, between rhythm guitar and lead guitar than at any other time in the Stones. The thing with musicians as fluid as Mick Taylor is that it's hard to keep their interest. They get bored, especially in such a necessarily restricted and limited music as rock and roll. That is the whole fascination with rock and roll and blues... how far you can take those limitations and still come up with something new."

Besides Taylor, another key element on 'Stop Breaking Down' was a keyboard performance by Ian Stewart. It was one of only three appearances on the album for the man who had been ejected from the Rollin' Stones for essentially looking too square. And he didn't seem much different now, looking like a rugby coach in his golf shirts amidst the storm cloud of sex, drugs and rock and roll that was Stones. Stu was a pillar of strength under such circumstances, and always welcome on band recordings. A song like 'Stop Breaking Down' was well-suited to his passionate boogie-woogie rolls. Stu was around for most of the sessions, but as a player he often just didn't seem interested. Most of the keyboard work was left to Nicky Hopkins. One time during the sessions in France, Johns suggested to Jagger that Stewart was perfect for a particular track. Why not have him play? "Oh, well, if you can." Jagger replied. When Johns approached Stewart, the road manager huffed: "No, I'm not playing for those fucking bastards anymore. They never fucking pay me! All the hits I've played on…" In the end, of course, Stu played.

"They had a very weird relationship," says Johns. "Stu dressed very straight, was very down to earth, loved the band, but when everything was going wrong Stu would stand firm in the centre of the eye of the hurricane. If they couldn't tell what they were doing, they'd ask Stu 'How's it going?' And he'd go: 'A load of fucking rubbish! Sounds like a bunch of fairies playing!' They'd laugh and pretend not to take any notice, but they would listen to Stu, because he'd been there forever."

BILLY PRESTON AND HIS MIGHTY ORGAN GRACED ALBUMS BY BOTH THE BEATLES AND THE STONES.

SHINE A LIGHT

Mick Jagger was once asked in the pages of *Creem* magazine if he would rather have been born a black man. "Yes, perhaps so," the singer replied, if only half-seriously. Blues, reggae, R&B, rock and roll – all of them had come out of the African experience, and all would forever fascinate Jagger and the Stones. Yet by 1971, the band was no longer simply copying the examples of Muddy Waters and James Brown and Chuck Berry. On *Exile On Main Street*, the Rolling Stones were playing music that still owed much to those forefathers, but it was also a sound they had made indelibly their own. There is an ease and understanding demonstrated on this album. Tracks like 'Shine A Light' and 'Let It Loose' reveal gospel elements that are noticeably earthier and deeper. A profound spirituality is at work within the harmony vocals that was missing on the lush chorale sounds of such earlier recordings as 'Salt Of The Earth' and 'You Can't Always Get What You Want.' With 'Shine A Light', the Stones leaned heavily on the organ sounds of Billy Preston, who was a prominent collaborator during the band's albums and tours of the early 1970s. "He had that gospel feel, you know, which Nicky didn't have," says Johns, who worked with Preston years earlier for the keyboardist's first solo sessions for the Beatles' Apple label. "He became pals with them. Billy was part of the scene back then because he'd been on Apple. Billy was always hanging out, and they liked the idea of that gospel thing."

SOUL SURVIVOR

The final moments of *Exile On Main Street* hinge on a sharp, edgy guitar riff that rolls on endlessly like a tape loop. Jagger may shout religiously above the fray, but it is the relentless chord pattern that keeps the tune in motion. That 'Soul Survivor' retains so much energy within such a limited – if dynamic – pattern says much about the rhythmic power in the hands of Keith Richards.

"If you want to understand Keith Richards' guitar playing, you watch him play snooker," says engineer George Chkaintz, who worked often with the Stones. "He has some difficulty in keeping any of the balls on the table. It's just extraordinary to see the way the point of decision happens with him. And he recognizes that as a weakness in his game of snooker. But it is absolutely explosive."

It's evident also in the guitarist's snaky, almost self-absorbed moves on stage, where Richards' instrument appears like just another physical part of himself – another appendage, much like John Coltrane's tenor sax. Richards is the sort of extremist who will strum a guitar until his fingers are bleeding all over the damn floor. It is that utter commitment that inevitably led to the twisted greatness of *Exile On Main Street*.

There would be more important peaks in the band's career, scattered across such albums as *Some Girls* and *Tattoo You*, and on selected tracks all the way up through the 1990s, despite the growing distractions of middle age and competing interests. But *Exile On Main Street* was undoubtedly the high water mark for the Rolling Stones. And what came after would never mean *quite* so much.

GOATS HEAD SOUP

Recorded	November 1972 to June 1973, Dynamic Sound, Kingston, Jamaica; The Doelen, Rotterdam, The Netherlands.
Produced by	Jimmy Miller.
Musicians	The Rolling Stones: Mick Jagger (vocals, acoustic guitar, harmonica, piano), Keith Richards (guitars, vocals, bass guitar), Mick Taylor (electric, acoustic, slide guitar, bass guitar, backing vocals), Charlie Watts (drums), Bill Wyman (bass guitar) Additional musicians: Nicky Hopkins (piano), Billy Preston (piano, organ, clavinet, percussion), Ian Stewart (piano), Bobby Keys (saxophone), Jim Price (saxophone), Jim Horn (flute), Chuck Findley (trumpet), Anthony "Rebop" Kwaku Baah (percussion), Pascal (Nicolas Pascal Raicevic) (percussion), Jimmy Miller (percussion).

DANCING WITH MR D

100 YEARS AGO

COMING DOWN AGAIN

DOO DOO DOO DOO DOO (HEARTBREAKER)

ANGIE

SILVER TRAIN

HIDE YOUR LOVE

WINTER

CAN YOU HEAR THE MUSIC

STAR STAR

IN WITH THE IN-CROWD: MICK JAGGER, DAVID BOWIE AND LOU REED KEEP THE BUBBLES FLOWING.

Witness as a new era begins for the fabulous Rolling Stones, a band whose legend was secure, and a band with nothing left to prove. Or so they believed. Jagger and Richards had entered the 1970s as one of the most powerful forces in rock, riding a crest of popular and critical acclaim for their every move, their every guitar riff and inflammatory lyric. Now what? Decay. The brilliant recklessness that had made *Exile On Main Street* such a profound and chilling return to the rawest blues and country imaginable had all of a sudden descended into rock-star befuddlement.

Goats Head Soup was not without its charms. A handful of tracks do shine through the haze, but the Stones had clearly fallen prey to distractions of one type or another. By now, Jagger had lost whatever connection he might have had with the middle-class Bohemianism that had guided his best early work, succumbing instead to the alarming "Jet-set" world of Lady Bianca. And what should have been a continuation of the band's most creative period was seriously hobbled by the further encroachment of heroin into the life of Richards. It was not simply decadence that knocked the Stones off-balance, but a sudden lack of will. In 1973, the attitude of the Glimmer Twins seemed to be saying "we've done it". Jagger later described the general mood of the band as "...general malaise. I think we got a bit carried away with our own popularity and so on. It was a bit of a holiday period."

Consequently, a mild atrocity like the new album's 'Dancing With Mr D' only demonstrated a failure of the imagination, leaning heavily on old ideas about evil and danger that had inevitably lost their edge the third or fourth time around. However, the mystery is why this deterioration came so soon after the band's creative peak, even if they were hardly the only major artists from the 1960s to stumble awkwardly into the new decade. But although John Lennon's *Mind Games* and Paul McCartney's *Red Rose Speedway* were both arguably their weakest albums, this was hardly true of their entire generation. Pete Townshend remained an ambitious voice, confirmed by the Who's recording of *Quadrophenia*. And the epic Led Zeppelin had emerged from the ashes of the Yardbirds to create a sound and vision of ominous power that even the Stones could not deny. The title of "World's Greatest Rock And Roll Band" was already beginning to ring somewhat hollow.

"This album will be less freaky, more melodic than the last one," Jagger promised *Rolling Stone* magazine in January 1973, during the making of *Goats Head Soup*. "We've recorded a lot of fast numbers already, maybe too many."

Fast or slow hardly mattered. When the Stones arrived in Jamaica for the *Goats Head Soup* sessions, heroin was the increasing obsession of Keith and other members of the Stones' entourage. The Stones had sought the isolation of Jamaica to escape the distractions of home, to allow them to work without interruption. But drug habits were harder to shake. "Consequently, those sessions weren't quite as much fun," Johns remembers now. "And there are a couple of examples on there where just the basic tracks we kept weren't really up to standard. People were accepting things perhaps that weren't up to standard because they were a little higher than normal. But there still are some fantastic things on there. There really are some jolly good moments."

The band and crew shared a hotel in Kingston, an old mansion called the *Terra Nova*, which was the family home of Island Records founder Chris Blackwell. They all ate breakfast together, but it wasn't quite a repeat of the communal feeling of the *Exile On Main Street* sessions in the South of France. Bobby Keys, for one, had been left behind – he would overdub his sax parts later. Sessions were recorded at Dynamic Sound Studios, a facility run by bandleader and producer Byron Lee, and where reggae singer Jimmy Cliff recorded his big-selling *Wonderful World, Beautiful People* album. But

"I THINK WE GOT CARRIED AWAY WITH OUR OWN POPULARITY."
MICK JAGGER

Goats Head Soup failed to tap into the rich musical legacy surrounding the Stones in Jamaica. In 1973, Bob Marley and the Wailers would release the politically charged reggae albums *Catch A Fire* and *Burnin'*, featuring a deep rhythm that wouldn't infect the Stones' sound until 'Luxury' the following year. After that, reggae would remain a permanent part of their repertoire.

Johns was sent ahead to Jamaica before the sessions to prepare the studio for the Stones' arrival. He discovered a good working area, but also a control room that was less than state-of-the-art. Speakers were strangely positioned, there were no sound screens to separate individual musicians, no grand piano or Hammond B3 organ, and some of the equipment was inadequate for the band's needs. Nonetheless, the studio's management agreed to provide the improvements, and Johns returned home. "Of course, I show up with the band two months later and none of this shit's been done," Johns says. "They work on a completely different time scale down there. After we were down there for two or three months, some of these things started to appear. So on the last day we had everything, when it was too late."

More disturbing was a vibe of violence that seemed to hover over the studio. "My assistant was telling of these nightmares about these guys hacking each other to death in the studio with these fucking machetes when they have arguments," says Johns. "The bass player would go over to his bass case and he'd have a machete, the other guy would have a fucking gun, and they'd go at it."

The Stones entourage suffered their own taste of that violence one night about six weeks into the recording, when a man with a knife broke into Bill Wyman's hotel room. The intruder demanded money and ordered Wyman underneath the bed. He then raped Wyman's longtime girlfriend, Astrid Lündstrom. Minutes later, Johns heard a knock on his door. It was Astrid. "Oh Andy, you'll never guess," she told Johns. "I've just been raped!"

Alarming news, and yet she seemed so clear-headed, says Johns, who was standing shoeless and in his shorts in the doorway. The engineer immediately grabbed some heavy object to use as a weapon and ran outside and down the road, cutting his feet on broken glass. But the rapist had escaped across the lawn in another direction. "Bill, obviously, was totally freaked because he'd had to lie under the bed while all of this went on," says Johns. "If he had done anything the guy would have cut his fucking head off. He really didn't have any fucking choice. It was a tough thing. It was another Rolling Stones thing. Shit like that was always going on. There was always something bizarre happening. There were some very unfair comments like 'Why didn't Bill do something? What a fucking weed!' Which I thought was totally uncool and uncalled for."

That kind of tension was often felt elsewhere within the band as, for the first time, Jagger and Richards began to drift apart. Keith was lost to drugs, Jagger to high society. In celebration of his glittery lifestyle, the singer would soon have a diamond planted into his front tooth. Marvellous!

"Throughout most of the seventies, I was living in another world from him," Richards told Kurt Loder in 1987. "I didn't blame him – he'd earned the right to do whatever he wanted. It was just that I couldn't relate to that… it kind of got up my nose a bit, that jet-set shit and, like, the flaunting of it. But he's a lonely guy, too. He's got his own problems, you know?"

Bill and Astrid moved into another hotel, and the sessions continued. The ultimate result was little more than a few energetic singles, and an album that inadvertently documented the uncertain focus of a once-great unit. Time was also an issue. While the Stones spent a year working on *Exile On Main Street*, the band this time was churning out the material much faster. Among the songs recorded just in their first month in Jamaica were 'Angie', 'Star Star' and 'Coming Down Again'. Also recorded during this same period was 'Waiting On A Friend', which wouldn't emerge until 1981's *Tattoo You*.

"I didn't think there was any one song on there that really stood out," says Bobby Keys, whose saxophone solos were not enough to lift the album's spirits. "I thought *Goats Head Soup* was kind of bland, shall I say, after *Exile On Main Street*."

Goats Head Soup would also mark the final appearance of Jimmy Miller as producer. When it came time for the Stones to record *It's Only Rock And Roll* the following year, his services were no longer required. It was the end of an important era for the band, which had recorded its greatest works, from *Beggars Banquet* to *Exile On Main Street*, with the producer. "When they first started working with him, he was a lot of help," Johns says of Miller. "Then after a year or two, they kind of used Jimmy for what they wanted, and learned Jimmy's tricks, and started shutting him out a bit. So by the time of *Exile On Main Street* they weren't listening to Jimmy very much, and it did him in. They weren't really being rude, but they would ignore him a lot more than he would have liked."

It would be a near-tragic fall for Miller, the Brooklyn-born percussionist and producer who had co-authored the Spencer Davis Group's 'I'm A Man' and produced classic albums by Traffic and Blind Faith. He would produce

"I THOUGHT GOATS HEAD SOUP WAS KIND OF BLAND, SHALL I SAY, AFTER EXILE ON MAIN STREET*"* BOBBY KEYS, SAXOPHONIST

only a handful of records over the next two decades, before his death from liver disease in 1994. After the Stones, Miller worked with the likes of Motorhead and Johnny Thunders. Hardcore characters to be sure. But the Stones had left him shaken and forever changed. "Jimmy," Keith later told *Crawdaddy* magazine, "went in a lion and came out a lamb. We wore him out completely. Same with Andrew Loog Oldham. Burned out like a light bulb. Andrew wanted to be Phil Spector, meanwhile I'm screwing his wife, nobody gives a shit and it's just… just ridiculous." Miller was neither the first nor the last casualty of the Rolling Stones.

DANCING WITH MR D

Here comes Mick Jagger, a man of unquestionable wealth and taste, who by 1973 had indeed been around for many a long, long year. Stolen many a man's soul and faith? Maybe. But if anyone still believed that Mr J was in fact a sympathetic soldier for Satan, then the cartoonish 'Dancing With Mr D' must have been very enlightening indeed.

It's not a bad rock track by any standard other than their own, but the song inevitably suffers from comparison to 1968's chilling 'Sympathy For The Devil', which examined the darker corners of the human soul across a riveting samba beat. In those days, Jagger boasted of dark events from history, such as war, assassination and crucifixion. The effectiveness of the song could be measured by the numbers of listeners who truly feared that Jagger was promoting black magic and violence. By contrast, 'Dancing With Mr D' is a tale best told on Halloween. Mick sings of traipsing around a graveyard, and being confronted by Mr D himself, a big-shot with a necktie made of human skulls – images more appropriate to the likes of horror novelists H.P. Lovecraft or Clive Barker. Nothing to fear here.

On 'Sympathy For The Devil', Jagger taunted his listeners with "Pleased to meet you, hope you guessed my name". This time, Jagger breathlessly sings, "Now I know his name, he's called Mister D, and one of these days he's gonna set you free." Silly, although no more ridiculous than the theatrics of Alice Cooper from the same era or the laughable death metal bands that emerged in the 1980s. At least '…Mr D' rocked convincingly.

For the Jamaican 'Dancing With Mr D' sessions, the Stones once again travelled down that dark road to the ominous funk of a sharp Keith Richards riff, a sound that later bands such as the Black Crowes would imitate endlessly. By now, though, this was little more than coasting for the vampire guitarist. The riff's arch tone hints at evil, but never fully delivers.

Thus, the opening shot on *Goats Head Soup* at once represented everything that was right and wrong with the Rolling Stones in the middle of the 1970s. The band's continued ability to conjure up at least a handful of driving rock tunes was enough to make it a third straight number one album on both sides of the Atlantic. But critics only heard failure, finding professionalism where there had once been profound inspiration. It's a verdict with which the Stones themselves would later come to agree.

100 YEARS AGO

These were strange days for the Stones. With their rock and roll heroes of the fifties now virtually irrelevant and a new generation of pop voices fast emerging, the Stones stood in the early 1970s as lonely journeymen of rock. Was their best behind them?

Jagger seemed to ponder this question on '100 Years Ago', a dissatisfying funk rocker that still included lyrics of real soul-searching. Even if the Stones' music on *Goats Head Soup* was falling out of focus, Jagger proved he could still pen lyrics that cut directly to personal experience when he sang "Don't you think it's sometimes wise not to grow up?"

His vocals are slurred, laid across the fluid jazz-rock of Mick Taylor, mingling with the ultrahip clavinet melodies of Billy Preston. The music is launched promisingly with driving mid-tempo funk, but it never fully erupts, even during a Taylor solo windout that's buried too deep in the mix to connect. The Stones would have better luck with funk in subsequent years, probing that seething rhythm more convincingly with the later albums *Black And Blue* and *Some Girls*.

COMING DOWN AGAIN

This is Keith Richards at his most tough AND vulnerable. It's a sensuous declaration of self, and of an imperfect lifestyle of love he shows no interest in abandoning. And that's just the way it is, darlin'!

'Coming Down Again' opens with a lilting piano melody played by Nicky Hopkins, but quickly descends to a slow junkie's pace, rolling along Keith's lethargic wah-wah playing. Likewise, Keith's lead vocals emerge in an exhausted tone, far from the ragged euphoria of 'Happy'. He's joined by Mick on quiet harmonies. If Richards often let Mick do the talking on the raunchier cuts, here the guitarist shows he can be as nasty as he wants to be with sexual innuendo: "Slipped my tongue in someone else's pie".

The track would be hopelessly weighted down by its numbing pace if not for a pair of muted, overlapping sax solos by Bobby Keys at the bridge. Although Keys had been present for the recording of basic tracks for *Exile On Main Street* in Keith's basement in the South of France, his parts on *Goats Head Soup* would be added long after the Stones had left Jamaica. Keys explains: "Keith and Mick get together before they go into the studio and write. Their writing can consist of just coming up with little pieces, ideas, riffs here and there. They'll go in the studio and put something down. When they cut an album they cut quite a few tracks, and then go back and review it and see what fits together. And then they decide what needs strings or voices or horns or whatever. My part of the recording usually comes at the very tail end of it."

DOO DOO DOO DOO DOO (HEARTBREAKER)

'Doo Doo Doo Doo Doo (Heartbreaker)' is not exactly social commentary – at least not in the traditional sense. But Mick Jagger skillfully exploits some inflammatory subject matter to create the most potent rock track on *Goats Head Soup*. The song opens with a scene of urban violence, as New York City Police kill an unarmed youth in a case of mistaken identity. Jagger sings angrily "Heartbreaker with your forty-four, I wanna tear your world apart!" He goes on to describe a 10-year-old girl sticking hypodermic needles into her arm, only later to be found dead in an alley. It's all grist for Mick's pumped-up rock and roll shouting – his own view on the deeper implications of these matters is left inconclusive.

The power of the song owes much to the duelling guitar attack of Richards and Taylor, along with the driving piano of Billy Preston. But the element that finally uplifts the track is a fitting blast of horns arranged by trumpeter Jim Price and overdubbed later. It would mark Price's final appearance on a Stones

recording project. He would soon embark on a career producing the likes of Joe Cocker, Herbie Hancock and Wayne Shorter.

The song become a hit single in America, but the prospects of 'Doo Doo Doo Doo Doo (Heartbreaker)' were far from certain back in Jamaica. "The track was really out of tune," Andy Johns told journalist Craig Rosen in 1994. "Everyone was so out of it that instead of recutting the track, Keith spent four months trying to get the bass in tune, and there was no way to make it work, because the electric piano and the guitar were out of tune with each other. Things were getting a little fuzzy there."

ANGIE

'Angie' stands as one of the most tender ballads in the Stones catalogue. In 1973, that was almost like a throwback to another era. The delicate acoustic guitar, Jagger's wounded, yearning tone, the romantic subject, all had more in common with earlier Jagger/Richards compositions like 'As Tears Go By' than with the charged rock sound the band had perfected by the early 1970s. A song that was heartfelt AND pretty is not what most listeners now expected from a band best known for cynicism and danger.

There were early rumours that 'Angie' was dedicated to Angela Bowie, and her marriage to Jagger's new friend David Bowie. But a close reading of the song suggests something much closer to Jagger's personal experience. In a promotional video made for the song, Jagger is seen in white silky threads, singing "Baby, dry your eyes... ain't it good to be alive... they can't say we never tried".

It's a sentiment that could easily have been inspired by Jagger's relationship with Marianne Faithfull. Once considered among London's most daring artistic couples, their relationship had finally collapsed in 1969 after an endless storm of troubles, which included a miscarriage, repeated drug busts and an attempted suicide.

Whatever the source material, the song struck a chord with listeners. The single of 'Angie' hit No. 2 in the UK, and topped the charts in the US.

SILVER TRAIN

The Stones recorded 'Silver Train' at Island Studios in London, seemingly inspired to reconnect with some chugging blues rock. And who better to send the boys along than that erstwhile Stone, Ian Stewart? His spirited boogie-woogie keyboard work is joined here by the slippery bottleneck of Taylor and the frantic harp-playing of Jagger, who blows a stirring train whistle between lyrics describing another jolly encounter with a prostitute.

Hearing an early take of the song, Texan blues-rocker Johnny Winter was sufficiently smitten to record his own version. Appearing on his Still Alive And Well album of March 1973, Winter's take of 'Silver Train' hit the streets months before Goats Head Soup was released.

HIDE YOUR LOVE

Basic tracks for much of Goats Head Soup were recorded back in Jamaica, but the crucial overdubs of horns and vocals were largely completed in England. One day at Olympic Studios, Jagger was sitting at a piano, killing time between tracking sessions.

"He was banging away at the piano and it sounded really cool," remembers Andy Johns. "Fuck, I'm going to tape this, because we could turn this into something later, you know? I said 'Come on man, let's do a whole pass on that, because you can use this. This is a really good vibe.'"

Jagger continued playing his lumbering piano melody, a sound with roots in gospel, and not unlike some of the most casual bits and pieces of Exile On Main Street. Johns played the tape for Mick and Jimmy Miller a week later, and both agreed it was worth exploring further. Mick Taylor added a bluesy guitar lead, Miller a bass drum. Hand claps were also brought into the mix, as Jagger again adopted the tone of a country preacher, testifying to his woman, shouting and rhyming lyrics that often sound improvised: "Oh, babe, I'm sinking, I wanna cry, well I've been drinking, but now I'm dry."

A close listen reveals a small voice in the distance that sounds suspiciously like Jagger. Though his proper vocals were later overdubbed, his singing during the recording of the basic track had bled into the piano microphone. At last, a touch of *Exile On Main Street*'s recklessness.

WINTER

Winter' was the first track cut in Jamaica for *Goats Head Soup*, and one of two tracks on the album recorded without Keith Richards. This left the track wide open for the kind of fluid melodies Mick Taylor had first explored on 'Sway' and 'Moonlight Mile' from *Sticky Fingers*. Though a less inspired composition than those 1971 recordings, 'Winter' reaches for the same epic heights.

Mick Jagger sings here like a man cast adrift, yearning wistfully for a failed romance: "It sure has been a cold, cold winter, and the light of love is all burned out".

It's a rare moment of vulnerability from the singer, and it's played out against an epic soundscape of strings and guitar. Taylor's rich leadwork flows in and out of a lush bed of strings arranged by Nicky Harrison. As with 'Angie', the song stood in 1973 as a monument to the Stones' ability to craft a tender ballad, even as the band's overall sound and purpose seemed to unravel. Andy Johns today calls the song "one of the best things they ever did".

Apart from the song's musical value, 'Winter' also demonstrated a human side of Johns' rock and roll paymasters, in spite of their well-deserved reputation for bitchiness. Shortly, before travelling with the Stones to Jamaica, Johns was producing an album with Jack Bruce, with whom Johns shared an apartment on New York's Park Avenue. After a night of debauchery, Johns awoke to find one of his arms numb, and the feeling wasn't coming back. Johns told Jagger about his arm, and offered to bail out of the *Goats Head Soup* sessions. "That's bullshit," Jagger told him. "You're coming. Look, it's all in your head anyway. I bet you get better real soon." A few days into the sessions, and just as they were finishing 'Winter', the feeling in his arm returned.

MICK JAGGER TRIES HARD TO LOOK COOL BACK IN 1973.

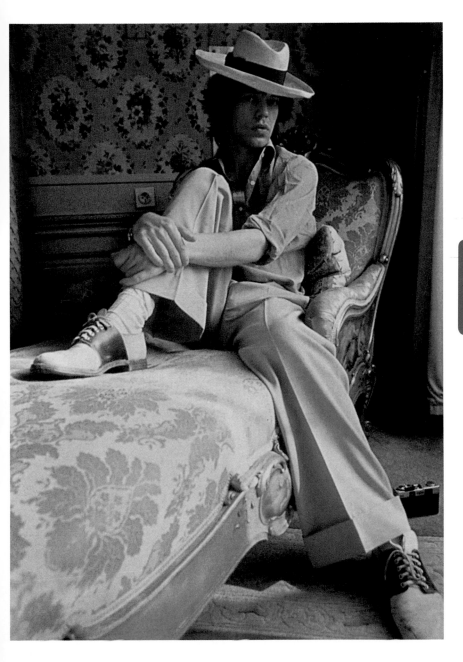

151

Several weeks later, the band and crew were working toward their Christmas break, which was still two weeks away. "Stu comes in, and he goes, 'I've got some really bad news: Your father is dying and he's asking to see you.' Mick put his arms around me and he says, 'We'll just stop now, you go home and see you're dad.'"

For Johns, whose father ultimately died of colon cancer, these were surprising signals of humanity from these notorious princes of darkness. "Which was unlike them. Their loyalty thing didn't stretch very far," Johns says with a laugh of the band he first met as the 14-year-old brother of engineer Glyn Johns. "They used to use people up very like a consumer society with their minions."

CAN YOU HEAR THE MUSIC

'Can You Hear The Music' sums up the problems that the Stones faced in the middle of the 1970s: self-indulgence, aimlessness and pointlessness. It would have fitted well within the psychedelic mishmash of 1967's *Their Satanic Majesties Request*, if that album hadn't been so energetic and memorable by comparison.

'Can You Hear The Music' opens with the delicate clamour of a ringing bell, percussion and the lilting flute of Jim Horn. They're soon swallowed up by spacey wah-wah guitar and Jagger moaning in a strangely nagging tone about his love for music. It emerges rather like an unfinished work-in-progress, with an odd clash of aesthetics. While *Their Satanic Majesties Request* built its psychedelic tripping on a solid pure-pop base, Jagger perversely chooses to sing here in a mush-mouthed bluesman's voice. It's an aggressively ethereal package best enjoyed with an unclear head.

Jagger can be heard singing "When you hear the music floating in the air, can you feel the magic?" That's an idealistic sentiment, coming as it did at a time when the music itself seemed to be losing the purpose and conviction the Rolling Stones once epitomized.

STAR STAR

Even groupies need an anthem. And who better qualified to document their comings and goings, their acrobatic skills and unique hygienic habits, than Mick Jagger? This was, after all, the same man listed as "number one on my far-fetched fuck list" by proto-groupie Pamela Des Barres. By 1973, groupies had long been part of the scenery. "Groupies? Oh yeah, man," Bobby Keys remembers. "In the early seventies? Like flies."

Des Barres was known throughout the sixties and seventies as Miss Pamela, a member of Frank Zappa's all-female GTOs (Girls Together Outrageous) "band" of fellow groupie chicks. Her eventual conquests included Jimmy Page, Keith Moon and Waylon Jennings, according to her 1987 book *I'm With The Band*. Her diary entry for November 25, 1969, reads: "I am extremely happy. I slept with Mr Jagger last night, and we got

153

IN THE 1970S JAGGER
FOUND HIMSELF
UNDER PERPETUAL
ASSAULT FROM
GROUPIES... AND
HE WASN'T TOO
UNHAPPY ΛBOUT IT.

along SO well; honesty, freedom and joy. Genuine. I helped him pack his seven suitcases, and he gave me some lovely clothes… The sexual experience was quite a joy."

So 'Star Star' was not just another song about girls. Originally entitled 'Starfucker', the tune told the story of the young girls whose men of choice are rock stars and movie stars. To the sounds of some rowdy Chuck Berry riffing, Jagger sings of a groupie "giving head to Steve McQueen", betting that she'll "get John Wayne before he dies".

Not everyone was over the moon about the song, however. Atlantic Records chief Ahmet Ertegun was aghast, and insisted that the title at least be changed to the innocuous 'Star Star'. Printed sheet music at the time changed the word "Starfucker" – used extensively in the chorus – to the laughably censored "Starbucker!

"At the time it was seen as incredibly outrageous," says Andy Johns. "To actually say 'FUCK' on a record. Nobody did that much, especially a record Mick knew was going to be a big record."

When *Goats Head Soup* was finally released in August 1973, 'Star Star' immediately won the attention of enraged feminists. In the context of so much of the Stones catalogue, 'Star Star' was seen as just another misogynistic attack. Miss Pamela may have called herself a "freewheeling feminist", but hers was not a brand of feminism that all women could rally around. Jagger was unrepentant: "That's real, and if girls can do that, I can certainly write about it because it's what I see," Jagger told *Rolling Stone* in 1978. "I'm not saying all women are star-fuckers, but I see an awful lot of them, and so I write a song called that. I mean, people show themselves up by their own behaviour, and just to describe it doesn't mean you're anti-feminist."

Jagger had worked up a demo of the song in Jamaica the night before recording, with Johns playing bass. The greatest challenge came months later, when an Atlantic representative paid a visit to Johns. Apparently, John Wayne had refused to give permission to include his name on the record. "Andy," the Atlantic man told him, "we've got to cover up this thing where it says John Wayne, otherwise we can't release the record." Johns then put a light repeat echo effect over the Wayne reference, and convinced the label rep that the average person would not be able to make it out. He lied. "Of course, when it came out you could still hear John Wayne," says Johns. "I was always happy about that." The CD reissue of *Goats Head Soup*, saw the band return to the original clearer version.

"GROUPIES? OH YEAH, MAN… IN THE EARLY 70S? LIKE FLIES!" BOBBY KEYS, SAXOPHONIST

"That's the only song with any slice of cynicism," Mick explained to *Rolling Stone* in 1973. "All the others are into beauty. It's very hard to write about those primitive emotions without being cynical about it – that's when you sound old. I mean, if you can't go into a coffee shop and sort of fall in love with every glass of coffee, and listen to the jukebox – that's difficult to portray in a song."

The controversy did not end with the album release. When the Rolling Stones went on tour in 1975, Jagger's performance of the song was accompanied by a giant inflatable phallus, much to the horror of proper authorities everywhere. "Police chiefs were waiting for it all over America," Keith Richards said later. "It was like a dare."

The band's willingness to document their lifestyle only went so far, however, which acclaimed photographer and film-maker Robert Frank discovered when he made his own brutal documentary of the band's 1972 tour. Entitled *Cocksucker Blues* (after an unreleasable song of the same name recorded by the Stones), the film captured a world of sex and drugs in graphic fashion. *Cocksucker Blues* also captured moments of musical euphoria, including a duet of Mick Jagger and Stevie Wonder performing 'Satisfaction'. More notorious, however, were scenes aboard their private tour jet, which showed the road crew stripping several groupies naked. After seeing the finished product, the Stones refused to allow the release of the film.

Cocksucker Blues has been seen infrequently ever since, mainly at unannounced screenings at small independent theatres and on college campuses. "What goes on on the tour was worse than what you see," Frank said at a 1976 screening. The tour, he continued, "was a hard trip to survive, but I was never disgusted. I didn't follow the whole tour – you get involved in a trip like this and you get so strung out it's impossible to work… and it shows. I'm told that Keith Richards liked the film, but his attitude is, he doesn't really care. He liked it better than Jagger."

Among such attempts to document the everyday debauchery of life with the Stones, it's those moments with the groupies on the airplane that remain the most memorable. "That wasn't typical. That was staged," insists Bobby Keys, a regular presence on most Stones tours during the 1970s. "Those chicks were brought on by a couple of the guys who handled the luggage. Robert Frank was wanting some material for his movie. That shit didn't really happen. It doesn't portray a totally wrong impression, but we didn't carry chicks around all the time, grab 'em up, take 'em on a plane and take their clothes off."

IT'S ONLY ROCK 'N' ROLL

Recorded	November 1973, February to May 1974, Musicland Studios, Munich, Germany; Rolling Stones Mobile/ Stargroves, Newbury, Berkshire; Ronnie Wood's home studio, Richmond, Surrey; Island Studios, London.
Produced by	The Glimmer Twins.
Musicians	The Rolling Stones: Mick Jagger (vocals, guitar), Keith Richards (guitars, backing vocals, bass guitar), Mick Taylor (electric/acoustic/slide guitar, backing vocals, synthesizer, congas, bass guitar), Charlie Watts (drums), Bill Wyman (bass, synthesizer). Additional musicians: Nicky Hopkins (piano), Billy Preston (piano, clavinet), Ian Stewart (piano), Ray Cooper (percussion), Charlie Jolly (tabla), Ed Leach (cowbell), Blue Magic (backing vocals), Kenney Jones (drums), Willie Weeks (bass guitar), David Bowie (backing vocals), Ronnie Wood (12-string acoustic guitar and backing vocals).

IF YOU CAN'T ROCK ME

AIN'T TOO PROUD TO BEG (WHITFIELD/HOLLAND)

IT'S ONLY ROCK 'N' ROLL (BUT I LIKE IT)

TILL THE NEXT GOODBYE

TIME WAITS FOR NO ONE

LUXURY

DANCE LITTLE SISTER

IF YOU REALLY WANT TO BE MY FRIEND

SHORT AND CURLIES

FINGERPRINT FILE

Why argue with success? In 1974, the magnificent Rolling Stones were the most beloved, feared, studied, praised and hated rock and roll band in the universe. *Goats Head Soup* was their third consecutive transatlantic No. 1 album, with more destined to come. They were the kings of rock, the potentates of pop, sitting pretty on a throne so secure that not even the Who or Led Zeppelin could claim it.

But the Stones knew better. Or at least Mick did. The singer probably hadn't been fully satisfied by a Stones record since *Let It Bleed*. Soon enough he would realize (and speak about it openly) that *Goats Head Soup* was the band's weakest album since 1967's *Their Satanic Majesties Request*. At least they were still trying in those crazy psychedelic days, making a record that is still worth a listen as a failed crackpot experiment gone half-wrong. Now they were beginning their second decade as a band, too often just going through the motions and hoping their ideas would be enough when execution failed them.

It's Only Rock 'N' Roll offered some improvement, a slight glimmer in the morass that the Stones had allowed themselves to become. Engineer Andy Johns remembers the sessions for the album as being even more submerged in drugs than *Goats Head Soup*, but there was a more consistent energy at work here. The hooks are sharper and the playing is more animated. Junior partner Mick Taylor's typically elegant playing on 'Time Waits For No One' is filled with troubled assurance and subtle regret. Not that the entire album reaches those heights.

It's Only Rock 'N' Roll is a great title for a concept album the Rolling Stones were uniquely qualified to make but never did. Instead, it's just the band following their usual formulas once again. Jagger does touch on the possibilities on the title track, briefly exploring the sick love-hate relationship the band had developed with its audience – "If I could stick a knife in my heart, suicide right on stage, would it satisfy ya?" But the possibilities are largely left unfulfilled. Best leave the concept albums to Pete Townshend.

A full recovery would not come to the Rolling Stones until *Black And Blue* the following year. But who would notice anyway? Many fans had undoubtedly preferred *Goats Head Soup* to the rough-hewn mess of *Exile On Main Street*, which at least had a little of the slick good-time boogie in the form of 'Doo Doo Doo Doo Doo (Heartbreaker)'. This meant that Keef could continue chopping out the same brand of riff-rock he mastered with 'Jumpin' Jack Flash' and 'Brown Sugar', even if the time to move on had long since passed.

"I DON'T KNOW THAT MICK TAYLOR EVER REALLY FIT IN."

GEORGE CHKIANTZ, ENGINEER

IN 1974, 31 WAS A
GRAND OLD AGE
FOR A ROCK STAR.
BUT DID MICK
REALLY THINK HE'D
STILL BE DOING
THIS MORE THAN 30
YEARS LATER?

In truth, Keith's worsening drug habits prevented much else, but the ramifications were growing ever more profound. His pal Gram Parsons had just overdosed in the California desert. Overindulgence, too, was partially to blame for the recent banishment of producer Jimmy Miller. And now Keith and Anita were banned from entering France for two years and each fined 5,000 francs, the result of a bust at Richards' villa in the South of France.

Trouble also brewed elsewhere in the band. Creative frustration had finally led Bill Wyman to release *Monkey Grip*, his first solo album, the previous May. More serious, however, was Mick Taylor's growing estrangement from the band, just as he had begun to assert himself. His guitar playing had deeply impacted the direction of the Stones over the previous five years, but he had only been awarded one co-writing credit – 'Ventilator Blues' from *Exile On Main Street*. And the guitarist had grown increasingly particular about how he played. During album sessions at Musicland Studios in Munich, Germany, Taylor often arrived early to record a bass overdub or try some other idea he had for a track. Keith usually erased them later.

"I don't know that Mick Taylor ever really fit in," remembers George Chkiantz, who engineered the overdubs for the album back in England. "In a sense, he was almost more of an outsider than Nicky Hopkins." In Munich, Johns remembers the Stones playing at a session when Richards suddenly turned to Taylor and said, "Fuck you! You play too loud. You're really good live, but you're no good in the studio. So you can play later."

Johns and Taylor were about the same age, in their mid-twenties, and had by then spent a lot of time together, most recently hanging out during the 1973 European tour and at the Jamaica sessions for *Goats Head Soup*. In Munich, Johns says, "He was whining and moaning: 'I never get to do what I want, and I don't think I'm going to be able to do this much longer'. And I'm going, 'What are you crazy?! You're going to quit the Stones? You're out of your fucking mind!'"

Before *It's Only Rock 'N' Roll* was finished, Johns' own heroin problem had grown so severe that he wasn't invited back to the sessions after the holiday break. He eventually went to work for Jack Bruce, formerly singer and bassist with Cream, who was then organizing a new band. Johns called Taylor. "Come on man, you've been talking about this for ages, quitting the band," he told Taylor, who was preparing to leave again for Munich to begin work on another album. "Come and play with Jack! It's the real thing! Jack's a genius and so are you!"

So Taylor quit the Rolling Stones. He released a statement to the press: "The last five-and-a-half years with the Stones have been very exciting, and proved to be a most inspiring period. And as far as my attitude to the other four members is concerned, it is one of respect for them, both as musicians and as people. I have nothing but admiration for the group, but I feel now is the time to move on and do something new."

For Taylor, the quiet, blond, young blues virtuoso, his exit from the Stones was inevitable. It was also a brutal career choice. "He would have left anyway," says Johns. "But the timing of it was obviously that my phone call instigated it. It was the worst thing I ever did. It wasn't a smart move… though they were jolly surprised when he quit. What is he insane? No one's ever left us before!"

The Stones' public reaction was somewhat more diplomatic. Jagger told *Rolling Stone*, "I'm sorry to see him go, but I think people should be free to do what they want to do. I mean, it's not the army, it's a sort of rock and roll band." In 1995, however, he added, "I think he found it difficult to get on with Keith."

THE FACES HAD THEIR VERY OWN "KEEF" IN THE FORM OF RONNIE WOOD *(CENTRE)*.

Mick Taylor's solo career never fully took off after that. The supergroup with Jack Bruce turned into "this miserable heroin festival, and nothing really much came of it," says Johns. Just a tour and little else. Taylor has since recorded a handful of eclectic albums, both under his own name and as a sideman to others. He made an appearance on Keith Richards' first solo album – 1988's *Talk Is Cheap* – and he was invited to join the Stones for their 1989 induction into the Rock and Roll Hall of Fame. The decline of his own fame with contemporary audiences can't erase a well-earned legacy as a key player on some monumental rock albums.

Young Mick was gone, but a clue to the future Stones was already planted within the title track of *It's Only Rock 'N' Roll*, which had been recorded at the home studio of Ronnie Wood of the Faces. But the album was still very much rooted in the early seventies. The band's cover of the Temptations' 'Ain't Too Proud To Beg' rolled with energy and bad attitude, adding to what amounted to a decent party record from the 1974 monsters of rock.

Of course, coming from a band with such a rich history, an album like *It's Only Rock 'N' Roll* could only be seen as something of a disappointment. It was surely more than a mediocrity, yet it contained fewer surprises than we had come to expect by the beginning of the 1970s.

IF YOU CAN'T ROCK ME

Enter the Glimmer Twins, producers extraordinaire. Maestro Andrew Loog Oldham was by now a fading memory, and poor Jimmy Miller a forced evacuee. Which left *It's Only Rock 'N' Roll* in the hands of Jagger and Richards themselves, officially in charge of producing a Stones album for the first time since the band had been left to their own devices on *Their Satanic Majesties Request*. Although a dubious legacy, the duo had learned much in the years since, having grown seasoned and sophisticated with time, as befitting their nom de plume.

These were men of wealth and taste. Certainly the Glimmer Twins knew what they were doing, launching the album with 'If You Can't Rock Me', a song of great sonic urgency in its opening moments. Jagger shouts frantically of being on stage, lusting for the crowd of women gathered in the front rows. It's just a few hours of warmth and love he needs tonight, not marriage or a lasting romance. To these ladies of "leather and lace" he makes his standard offer – if it's not you who indulges "somebody else will".

The song is carried by the seething force of Jagger's vocals and the pounding of Charlie Watts, and is a vast improvement over much of *Goats Head Soup*. Except that the winding, grinding groove never quite falls into focus. Richards and Taylor scrape their guitars in search of a memorable riff, but barely end up with even a middling melody. Is this how Jimmy Miller would have started things off?

IT'S ONLY ROCK 'N' ROLL (BUT I LIKE IT)

No band born in the 1960s pushed the boundaries of taste and decorum further than the Rolling Stones, a band forever tarnished by Oldham's bad press. Sex, drugs, revolution, Satanism, violence and decay – all subjects explored in extremis by "The World's Greatest Rock And Roll Band". But even Mick Jagger had to wonder if maybe things had been carried too far, serving an insatiable audience hungry for endless shock and titillation.

The Stones had seen their early shows erupt into dangerous rioting, been mobbed in the streets, had young girls fling their bodies at their moving limos, had to literally run for their lives. Meanwhile, their worst experiences – the drug busts, car wrecks, the death of Brian Jones, Altamont – were somehow interpreted in the most romantic light possible, marking just another chapter in the Stones' great outlaw legend.

At first glance, 'It's Only Rock 'N' Roll (But I Like It)' appears as just another light-hearted anthem celebrating the music. And yet Jagger sounds both in command and truly spooked as he contemplates the entertainment value of self-mutilation and public suicide. Perhaps real tears and insanity would also be amusing. "Would it be enough for your teenage lust? Would it help to ease the pain?" These are heavy questions, even if Jagger is playing them mostly for laughs, and partly as a jibe, perhaps, at the new generation of exhibitionist glam-rockers and proto-punks – but imagine these same lyrics in the hands of Iggy Pop.

Jagger had always talked disdainfully of rock, as if he regretted dropping out of university and the respectable life he might have led. And the very title of the song and album was taken as an insult by some listeners for whom rock and roll provided transcendence, not just cheap thrills. Yet between the wisecracks are haunting observations of the demanding relationship between audience and rock star, where the threshold of expected behaviour is raised ever higher.

Although Jagger and Richards were the song's credited composers, 'It's Only Rock 'N' Roll (But I Like It)' was first sketched out by Mick and Ronnie Wood, the ever-playful guitarist with the Faces. The Stones had known Wood since he was a baby guitarist hanging around the Crawdaddy and Marquee clubs. He was now successfully partnered with singer Rod Stewart, and together they had left their own trail of rock and roll debauchery with the Jeff Beck Group and then the Faces.

Engineer George Chkiantz was quickly summoned one night to Wood's home studio in Richmond, where he found Jagger and Wood both strumming acoustic guitars. The basic track was recorded with Willie Weeks on bass, and a brutal crash of drums and cymbals by Kenny Jones of the Faces. The final recording was finished in Munich, where Richards added sharp bursts of Chuck Berry-style riffing. Ian Stewart's piano can be heard in the distance.

Although it was Wood's first appearance with the Stones it's more than likely that his own parts were erased by Keith. This could explain Wood's credit as "inspiration" for the song, but nothing more.

The final result is a song of relentless rock and roll crunch, but the central instrument here is Jagger's voice, shouting his explosive cautionary tale.

TILL THE NEXT GOODBYE

Bright acoustic guitars bathe a soft vocal melody from Mick Jagger, who manages to create a folksy groove touched with romance and regret. 'Till The Next Goodbye' is a troubled Manhattan love story, with vague suggestions of a rendezvous at some local coffee shop or movie theatre. The tale of endless tears and goodbyes is told through a smooth blend of guitar and Nicky Hopkins' piano. It's far from the rugged country-folk of *Beggars Banquet*, but the song sparks to emotional life at the chorus with Jagger's words of warmth and longing. The Stones may have fallen out of sync with the casual greatness they enjoyed only two years before with *Exile On Main Street*, but 'Till The Next Goodbye' demonstrated that the band was still capable of a quiet grace.

TIME WAITS FOR NO ONE

Mick Taylor changed the Rolling Stones. But not forever, and not in the way that Brian Jones and his teenage blues fanaticism continued to haunt the band well into the 1980s. Taylor's influence depended entirely on his presence, and the graceful, intricate lead work that for five crucial years took the Stones into new musical territory. For all the grumbling from rock and blues purists about the guitarist's occasional self-indulgences, 'Time Waits For No One' demonstrated his profound strengths as a guitarist. This was a sound as much about subtlety as rock muscle. And once Taylor was gone, the Stones would rarely pass this way again.

During these final days with the Stones, Taylor's playing did often feel detached from the rest of the band, and undoubtedly reflected the guitarist's deteriorating relationship with the others. But a connection was made with 'Time Waits For No One', as Taylor's graceful, almost rushed leads reflected the drama and breathless emotion of Jagger's lyrics. If the playing had more to do with Carlos Santana than Chuck Berry, it still meshed seemlessly with Nicky Hopkins' cascading piano melodies and the steady tick-tock beat of Charlie Watts.

Jagger's message may seem an obvious one, but the note of regret in his voice sounds real. Nothing is safe from the passage of time, he warns, not man-made monuments, not a woman's face, not the Stones. "Hours are like diamonds," Jagger sings. "Don't let them waste." In 1974, Jagger turned 30, a milestone once unthinkable for the modern rock star, though he was hardly alone – not with the ex-Beatles still around, and grandpa Chuck Berry scoring his first No. 1 hit in 1972 with the ridiculous 'My Ding-A-Ling'. Yet it's unlikely that it was simply age that inspired these philosophical musings on wasted time. No one better illustrated his theme than Keith Richards, now spending what might have been his most productive years trapped in stupor and decay, bringing the Stones' chance at continued greatness down with him.

In time, Jagger acknowledged that the era of *Goats Head Soup* and *It's Only Rock 'N' Roll* were lost years for the band. Their inherent gifts meant that memorable music still emerged from the Stones even while they were coasting, but it was here that the band relinquished their position as rock and roll trailblazers. The Stones still came up with the odd thrill, and no act could draw a bigger crowd on the concert circuit. They continued to inspire a new generation of rockers in their own image, whether it was the glam-

MR TAMBOURINE
MAN: RAY COOPER
PERFORMS WITH
ELTON JOHN.

blues boogie of Aerosmith or the bitchy personality crisis of the New York Dolls. And the Stones would enjoy remarkable comebacks, such as 1978's *Some Girls* and 1981's *Tattoo You*. But the 1970s would ultimately belong to others, much as they had once shared credit for the 1960s with the Beatles. Even before the advent of punk, listeners and critics were already turning to a new wave of artists: David Bowie, Neil Young, Al Green, Bruce Springsteen, Bob Marley, all of them introducing new sounds and ideas to pop. Not even the late-eighties retro of the Black Crowes and other Stones wannabees could bring it back to the way it once was.

Basic tracks for 'Time Waits For No One' dated back to the *Sticky Fingers* sessions at Jagger's *Stargroves* mansion, but final overdubs for the entire album were done at London's Island Studios. Engineer George Chkiantz remembers that Watts commuted to the sessions by train, wearing pink-striped trousers while sharing the ride with crowds of businessmen in bowler hats and grey handlebar moustaches.

A song like 'Time Waits For No One' demanded a rich, layered texture to reflect the quasi-spiritual message. So one day Jagger announced he was bringing in a new percussionist named Ray Cooper. This came as surprising news to Chkiantz, who considered Jagger an exceptional percussionist himself, given to wild dance steps with the maracas behind the microphone. After all, who could possibly shake, rattle and roll more spectacularly than Mr Jumpin' Jack Flash? And Cooper's history playing in

Elton John's backing band wasn't the sort of thing to endear him to the rock and roll set. "No, no, you wait till you see this guy," Jagger told Chkiantz, clearly excited about the prospects. "You will not *believe* it. This is a treat for you as much as for anybody else."

Cooper soon arrived at Island for two efficient days of work, with his congas and tambourines, his various sticks, blocks, bones, bells, gongs, triangles and things. He was a tall man, with hair cut extremely short, practically shaved to the scalp. Cooper played it all, but it was his work on tambourine that was most astonishing. The man coaxed an amazing range of sounds from the thing, putting the simple instrument through an ordeal of shaking, pounding, tapping, caressing, thumping, knocking, coddling, cuddling, snuggling, nuzzling, whacking and jabbing.

"Let's face it, what do you do with a tambourine?" says Chkiantz. "Shake, shake, thwack! And this guy was getting a symphony out of the thing. He was just unbelievable, running his hands around the rim. His precision was just incredible. He'd actually tell you a story on this stupid bloody instrument. If you haven't seen it you've really missed out."

The percussionist's work appears all over *It's Only Rock 'N' Roll*, but it's within the lush mix of 'Time Waits For No One' that Cooper's presence is most felt. The final track is a lavish meditation on fate.

It isn't the album's most memorable tune – Keith's rockers were often best at sticking to your ribs – but there is something poignant in Jagger's message of regret, and his clear desire to push the Stones ever higher.

LUXURY

The rhythms of reggae had failed to penetrate the Stones' universe when the band recorded *Goats Head Soup* in Jamaica, but 'Luxury' suggests the band might have been paying attention after all. Not that this track has much in common with the Wailers, other than a certain hypnotic rhythm. Richards twists the genre to his own ends here, adding guitars that crunch more like the music of Chuck Berry than Bob Marley. The Stones would, of course, soon explore a more traditional reggae sound with 'Cherry Oh Baby' on *Black And Blue*.

On 'Luxury', Jagger adopts another of his notorious dialects. As his vocals slowly drift deeper into the mix, he sings as a man working hard to keep his woman and daughter out of poverty. Why must he spend his Sundays at the oil refinery while his millionaire bosses grow even richer?

IT'S A HARD LIFE FOR
KEITH RICHARDS
IN "THE WORLD'S
GREATEST ROCK AND
ROLL BAND".

DANCE LITTLE SISTER

Pray for Keith? Not at all! The man was merely indisposed. Try to ignore the image of walking, talking death, the head full of rotting teeth, the veins flooded with unfathomable toxins. He was, after all, a family man. Richards would never be caught strangling on his own vomit, drowning in a swimming pool, falling out a hotel window or choking on a ham sandwich. His heart would not explode in this decade, nor would he pass out on some inconvenient railroad tracks. This was no drug casualty, not really. Keith knew his limits. And if he seemed somehow diminished in the mid-seventies, Richards never once abandoned his role as key collaborator and Glimmer Twin.

Others have tried to be Keith, his bad example leaving a trail of rock-star bodies caught in its sway. In the end, even Johnny Thunders was proved an amateur. The implications of Keith's demon life seemed to be of little concern to the guitarist himself, depicted on the cover of *It's Only Rock 'N' Roll* as a dishevelled wreck, slouching in ill-fitting clothes. He was no longer the musician he had been on *Let It Bleed*, when Richards played most of the guitars and created a new, harrowing sound to close out the 1960s. That kind of clarity and musical ambition was inevitably clouded by continued drug use. But his ability to craft a flaming guitar riff never wavered, as the brutal opening to 'Dance Little Sister' demonstrated once more.

Leave the ethereal wispyness of 'Time Waits For No One' and other epics to Mick and Mick. There is no doubt which is the lead instrument on 'Dance Little Sister', no matter how busily Taylor twists his guitar to some excitable passages at the margins. Keith's rhythm guitar sends the Stones on a savage course, bolstered by a fierce pounding from Charlie and Stu's rolling bar room piano deep in the mix. Jagger vamps and seethes at the image of women in high heels and tight skirts and painted lips out on the town, urging them to dance and shake for him all night long.

'Dance Little Sister' has all the elements needed for the best kind of devil's music, and yet the song never fully erupts, never clicks into a perfect groove. Whether it was Keith's fading energy, uncertain band cohesion or some other cause, the Stones were no longer thriving musically as they once had.

In Munich, the Stones attempted to recreate the community vibe that had worked so well for 1972's *Exile On Main Street*. Band and crew shared the same hotel, just as they had done in Jamaica. "Everyone used to take their old ladies with them everywhere in those days," says engineer Andy Johns. "I'm not saying it was like a hippie thing back then. But when you were doing a project like that, it's not like it is now; there was a lot more sense of family and community and we're all in this together kind of a thing."

Johns remembers Ronnie Wood hanging out a bit, and jamming with Keith on Dobie Gray's 1973 hit 'Drift Away', a song Richards listened to every day for a month. The Stones abandoned that for the Temptations' 'Ain't Too Proud To Beg', an early high point for the album, recast with an echoing Richards riff. But not even these few moments of inspiration, and an attention-grabbing graffiti publicity campaign for the album, disguised the sound of a band in decay.

IF YOU REALLY WANT TO BE MY FRIEND

For a godless quintet of British rock stars, the Rolling Stones were surprisingly fluent in American gospel. 'If You Really Want To Be My Friend' is no match for the stirring likes of 'Let It Loose' from *Exile On Main Street*, but the Stones find a soulful groove here which is both relaxed and moving. With the air of a confessional, Jagger sings of love and trust across more than six minutes of spirited gospel. Mick Taylor erupts with a lead that is equal parts strength and melancholy. Vocal group Blue Magic add soothing harmonies, and Nicky Hopkins draws typically elegant harmonies from his piano. "Looking back at these albums, Nicky's contribution is enormous in my view," says George Chkiantz, who had watched Hopkins work with the Stones since 1967. "So many Stones tracks that we know and love are almost inconceivable without Nicky on them."

SHORT AND CURLIES

Ian Stewart was no roadie. He was the Stones' ambassador, their foul-mouthed stage manager, their closest comrade, their boogie-woogie conscience, a rock and roll gentleman and a committed golfer. But mainly he was a piano player. And 'Short and Curlies' was perfectly tailored to his purist rhythm and blues sensibility.

"He loved the band, hated what they were doing a load of the time and moaned about it," remembers Chkiantz. "But he was devoted to the band, and stuck with them through thick and thin." He had never expressed any lasting bitterness at being ejected from the early Rollin' Stones. And maybe it was for the best, since Stu's boogie-woogie sensibility might have clashed with some of the wilder musical turns explored by the Stones over the years. By standing outside the band, Stu could play only what he liked, and leave the rest to Nicky Hopkins. "He wasn't overly convinced by Nicky Hopkins' playing," Chkiantz says with a laugh. "He said, 'Do you really like that sort of thing?' Stu was one of the nicest guys. Wonderful character. I'm sure that if Stu wanted to play on something he had a way of making it known."

On 'Short and Curlies', Stu's piano is right out front, not buried in the mix, and it rolls with a boys-will-be-boys impishness. It's joined by the dual guitars of Richards and Taylor as Jagger sings of a man comically under the thumb of a woman. She's spent his money, crashed his car, and yet he can't (or won't) get away. "She's got you by the balls!" Naughty, haughty, sexist boogie-woogie heaven.

FINGERPRINT FILE

'Fingerprint File' was a clue to the coming funk of *Black And Blue*. The thumping bassline and wah-wah guitar owe something to the sounds of Hollywood blaxploitation films – such as *Shaft* and *Superfly* – not to mention Stevie Wonder, Sly Stone and the coming disco explosion. It's a fitting beat for Mick Jagger's private-eye paranoia, sounding the alarm for an age of diminished privacy.

"Some little jerk in the FBI is keeping papers on me six-feet high," Jagger sings, and he's not kidding. Revelations on the US government's extensive surveillance of John Lennon confirms whatever worries Jagger is expressing here – of the mountain of FBI paperwork on Lennon, sections remained classified even into the 1990s. His own history of drug arrests, supposed devil worship, and his association with any number of long-haired commie troublemakers undoubtedly made Jagger a threat to the "American way". So satellites, phone-taps, ultraviolet photography, G-Men and old-fashioned snitches have all got him feeling down and desperate.

The track would mark Mick Taylor's final appearance on a Stones album – at least until the vault-raiding *Tattoo You* – ending an important period for the band. The Rolling Stones soon found some renewed energy, resulting in the comeback albums *Black And Blue* and *Some Girls*. Guitarist Ronnie Wood, who was Taylor's replacement the following year, played in a style more like Keith Richards. Together, they traded riffs and rhythms and headed toward the 1980s with a more driving hard rock sound.

Some listeners would forever miss Taylor's fluid elegance. During the next decade, interviewers rarely failed to ask the Glimmer Twins to evaluate the different Stones eras: Jones versus Taylor versus Wood. They couldn't very well answer that their best years were behind them, but acknowledged the special achievements during Taylor's tenure, from 'Honky Tonk Women' to *Exile On Main Street*. These were monumental recordings for the Stones, and anything they created in the future would surely be judged against them.

A GREAT GUITARIST, BUT MICK TAYLOR WAS ALWAYS AN OUTSIDER IN THE ROLLING STONES.

BLACK AND BLUE

Recorded	December 1974 to February 1976, Musicland, Munich, Germany; Montreaux, Switzerland; Rolling Stones Mobile/Rotterdam, The Netherlands.
Produced by	The Glimmer Twins.
Musicians	The Rolling Stones: Mick Jagger (Vocals, percussion, guitar, electric and acoustic piano.) Keith Richards (guitar, vocals, Fender Rhodes, bass guitar), Charlie Watts (drums, percussion), Bill Wyman (bass guitar, percussion). Additional personnel: Ronnie Wood (guitar, backing vocals), Billy Preston (piano, backing vocals, string synthesizer), Harvey Mandel (electric guitar), Wayne Perkins (acoustic/electric guitar), Ian Stewart (percussion), Ollie Brown (percussion).

HOT STUFF
HAND OF FATE
CHERRY OH BABY (DONALDSON)
MEMORY MOTEL
HEY NEGRITA
MELODY
FOOL TO CRY
CRAZY MAMA

The day after Mick Taylor quit the Rolling Stones, Keith Richards sent a telegram. "Really enjoyed playing with you for the last five years," it read. "Thanks for all the turn-ons. Best wishes and love." Taylor cried when he read it. Such a touching note of goodwill, so generous and merciful. Or so it seemed. Some observers have interpreted its brevity to reflect a sarcastic send-off to the boy guitarist. It was, after all, just a telegram, not an essay. In any case, neither Jagger nor Richards were shaken enough by Taylor's departure to abandon plans for their next album. Sessions for what would become *Black And Blue* began according to schedule in Munich.

That meant the Stones were once again a quartet, just as they had been during the making of *Let It Bleed*. No one performed more heroically than Keith on that album, filling the gaps left by a quickly fading Brian Jones with music that was inventive, foreboding and alive. His guitar work on 'Gimme Shelter' and 'Midnight Rambler' carried the Stones to a new level of creative intensity in 1969. *Let It Bleed* had been 43 minutes of scorched vinyl, music thick with danger and enlightenment. No way Keith was up to that now, not in this season of smack. It was enough that he could still play at all, and still create those crucial four-chord riffs. So at the end of 1974, the Stones *needed* a second guitarist, someone to fill in the band's new empty spaces.

It would prove a hotly contested gig, and recording sessions for *Black And Blue* were all of a sudden transformed into auditions for Taylor's replacement. The Stones spent the next eight months jamming and recording endlessly with a long line of guitarists. The top candidates were British guitar hero Jeff Beck, Americans Harvey Mandel and Muscle Shoals session man Wayne Perkins, and, finally, Ron Wood of the Faces. Not a lot in common among that group. Beck, for one, had just released his acclaimed *Blow By Blow* album, an all-instrumental jazz-funk windout with little obvious connection to the rock and blues frenzy of his Yardbirds days, or even to the contemporary Stones. At the other end of the spectrum stood happy Ronnie Wood, rock and roller to the core, whose collaborations with Rod Stewart were a mixture of ragged joy (Faces albums) and focussed brilliance (Stewart's solo discs). The final version of *Black And Blue* would include playing by each of them... except for Beck, who is said to have insulted the legendary Stones rhythm section. His parts were erased.

The cross-section of styles and temperaments made *Black And Blue* the band's most eclectic batch of tracks since the late 1960s, opening with Harvey Mandel's astonishing hyperfunk on 'Hot Stuff'. The fluid lead lines of Wayne Perkins on 'Hand Of Fate' came closest to the sound of Taylor,

while Woody's rugged riffing on 'Hey Negrita' was most like Keith's. If replacing Brian Jones had seemed such an easy, an almost casual choice – a recommendation from John Mayall was almost enough – replacing Taylor was somewhat more agonizing. Just as Taylor's elegant blues leads had helped the Stones master a new sophisticated rock blend at the beginning of the decade, the choice of Keith's new sideman would obviously have long-term ramifications.

THE PRESENCE OF RONNIE WOOD ON SECOND GUITAR GAVE THE STONES A MUCH NEEDED BOOST OF VITALITY.

"Basically, the Rolling Stones are a two-guitar band, that's how they started off," Richards told *Crawdaddy*. "And the whole secret, if there is any secret behind the sound of the Rolling Stones, is the way we work two guitars together. As far as records go it's no big hassle for me not to have another guitar player 'cause I'm used to doing all the parts. It's just I *like* working with another player, that's the turn-on for me."

Perkins came achingly close to winning the gig, until Wood returned late to the *Black And Blue* sessions. He could finally be heard playing on three album tracks, compared to Wood's two, but Ronnie had long ago made a special connection with the band – and especially Keith Richards. Both Mick and Keith appeared on his *I've Got My Own Album To Do* solo LP in 1974, and the seeds of 'It's Only Rock 'N' Roll' were recorded at Wood's home studio that same year. Band folklore has it that Wood had actually been offered the job back in 1969, before the Stones settled on Taylor. Whether that's true or not, Wood was an easy fit in 1975, and a needed burst of positive energy in a band fraying at the edges from drug use and internal resentments.

"I loved Mick Taylor for his beauty," Bill Wyman said later. "He was technically really great. But he was shy, maybe like Charlie and me. Mick wasn't so funky, but he led us into other things. Ron is a bit like Keith, he takes us back. He's not such a fantastic musician, but he's more fun, got more personality."

But Woody wasn't about to abandon his mates in the Faces, even if Stewart's solo career had long since eclipsed his work in the band. A new Faces album and tour was already in the planning stages. So officially, at least, the guitarist signed up only as a temporary Rolling Stone, helping the band finish *Black And Blue*, posing for the dramatic album cover photograph by Hiro, and touring the US that summer. Then Ronnie would be back with the Faces again, he promised.

Of course, the Faces were already in the final stage of a sad breakup. Never as lauded as the Stones, they had only scored a handful of UK hits in their career, and only the rocking 'Stay With Me' had made an impression in the US. Furthermore, bass player and occasional vocalist Ronnie Lane had already quit. Both Stewart and Wood saw the end coming, and finally used each other's extracurricular activities as justification for their inevitable departures. The Faces were gone.

"Woody and Rod were like Mick and Keith," says singer-guitarist Bobby Womack, a longtime friend to both Wood and the Stones. "They were tight. And when Rod left, Woody had no other choice but to say, 'Well, the

Stones always wanted me, I'm going to go with them'." So it was, that on February 28, 1976, Ron Wood was announced as the newest member of the Rolling Stones.

The earliest sessions for *Black And Blue* marked a reunion between the band and engineer Glyn Johns, who had been the first to record the young Rollin' Stones in the early days. Later, Johns recorded such era-defining albums as *Beggars Banquet* and *Let It Bleed*, before drifting off into other projects and leaving the Stones to his younger brother, Andy.

His return to the Stones fold was the result of a preliminary agreement that Johns would receive a co-producer's credit on *Black And Blue*, unless he failed to finish the album for any reason. In December 1975, Johns and the band arrived in Munich. "We got on tremendously well and we cut an immense amount of material in a very short period of time, under extremely pleasant circumstances," Johns told Craig Rosen in 1994. "It was great for me to be back with them because I hadn't seen them for a while, and we were all extremely close friends for several years. That was really nice."

For Glyn Johns, the absence of Mick Taylor at the sessions was a welcome surprise. Although he acknowledged the guitarist's important role during a crucial stage of the Stones' career, he had grown increasingly finicky, contributing almost as much as Keith in the amount of time spent (and wasted) in the studio. "Frankly," Johns said, "I didn't get on with him very well."

So much else had changed within the Stones universe since Johns had last worked with them, recording tracks that later appeared on *Sticky Fingers* and *Exile On Main Street*. In Munich, Keith was still suffering from the death of his second son, Tara – named after Tara Browne, the young royal and scene-maker eulogized in the Beatles' 'A Day In The Life' – who had been born prematurely 10 days earlier. And Mick was battling a paternity suit with Marsha Hunt – a suit later settled out of court. Keith also had a brand new set of teeth, replacing his rotted junkie fangs with a row of pearly whites more appropriate to a jet-setting rock star. Meanwhile, Bill Wyman had just released his first solo album, *Monkey Grip*, and already had plans to release another, *Stone Alone*.

There was also the irritation of *Metamorphosis*, an album of barrel-scraping outtakes and misfires from the 1960s released by former manager Allen Klein. It was a collection best left on the shelves, and not even Andrew Loog Oldham's liner notes of loving beat poetry could disguise the weakness of what was inside. Balancing that atrocity was *Made In The Shade*, which gathered some of the band's best tracks of the new decade.

The most astonishing change within the Rolling Stones, at least for Johns, was the band's new willingness to work quickly. In Munich, the band managed to cut 11 tracks in 11 days, a dizzying pace against the agonizingly slow sessions that Johns remembered from London. But it wasn't to last. After the Christmas break, the Stones gathered in Rotterdam to continue work on *Black And Blue* in a rehearsal facility designed for symphony orchestras. The Rolling Stones Mobile unit was parked outside. This was Mick's idea to save money, but to Johns it made no sense at all.

"The whole environment in this place in Holland was not really right and extremely inconvenient," said Johns, who was growing irritated that recording time was being used for guitarist auditions. "I was parked in the street. They were on the third floor of this building. Every time I wanted to go and adjust a mike, I had to walk up four flights of stairs and down ten corridors. In the end, there was a misunderstanding between Keith and I which caused an argument from me. I lost my rag, and suppose it was years and years of nonsense that had built up… I said my piece and told the Rolling Stones they could go fuck themselves. That was the end of that."

At the time, Johns figured that the album was just about finished anyway. But the band still managed to spend several more months in the studio. For Johns, who has not worked with the Stones since, it was one big disappointment: "I've never listened to the record," he said later. "I'm sure they fucked it up."

US GUITAR WIZARD HARVEY MANDEL – DOES THIS MAN REALLY LOOK LIKE A ROLLING STONE?

177

HOT STUFF

Black And Blue opens with a jarring blast of high-tension funk, a sound that was unexpected and extreme coming from the "World's Greatest Rock And Roll Band" in 1976. Here, at last, was a sign of life from the embattled Rolling Stones, a band that had long since drifted into predictable, straight-ahead riff-rock. Inertia was now replaced by Mick's alarming first declaration of dance fever. Rock extremists were horrified. Were the Stones being swept up within a disco scene fast emerging from the

underground via international hits like Donna Summer's 'Love To Love You Baby'? Was rock dead?

Not while Keith Richards walked the earth. 'Hot Stuff' was not the enemy, but rather the Stones' twist on a classic funk groove, closer in spirit to James Brown and Sly Stone than to any of the slick disco tracks beginning to haunt the radio. The song was built around the high-pitched riffing of Keith, with melodramatic accents from the rumbling piano chords of Billy Preston. "Auditioning" guitarist Harvey Mandel sends flames across this heavy groove as Mick chants passionately about lives lived to a big beat, and improvising wildly to all those going broke in New York City that "I know you're tough!"

BY THE TIME *BLACK AND BLUE* WAS BEING RECORDED BILLY PRESTON HAD ALREADY FORGED A SUCCESSFUL SOLO CAREER FOR HIMSELF.

The track was recorded in March 1975 at Musicland Studios in Munich, where the Stones were augmented by percussionist Ollie E. Brown. "That sucker felt good that night," Brown says now. "It really came together that night."

If not all listeners were overjoyed at the prospect of the Rolling Stones "going disco", a song like 'Hot Stuff' was in fact a logical extension to the band's longtime commitment to the sounds of Black America. This was merely the Stones' mid-seventies take on what they had already witnessed during their first visits to the Harlem Apollo. 'Hot Stuff' was no more of a departure than the sudden mid-nineties interest in electronica and jungle beats by the likes of David Bowie and U2.

That wasn't the end of the matter, however. Even more controversial than these first moments of *Black And Blue* was the album's advertising campaign, which depicted a blonde woman tied up and covered in bruises. Feminists and many others were appalled at the image, which was soon scattered across billboards and magazine pages. "I thought it was quite funny," Richards told *Creem* magazine in 1979. "Trouble is, not too many people have a sense of humour, especially institutions... Goddamn it, a large percentage of American women wouldn't be half as liberated if it wasn't for the Rolling Stones in the first place, and people like us. They'd still be believing in dating, rings and wondering whether it was right to be kissed on the first date or not."

HAND OF FATE

No mistaking the sound behind 'Hand Of Fate' – the grinding electric guitars, the tough, driving rhythm. The opening riff passage was clearly Keith's, but there was a new clarity and energy here. On *Goats Head Soup* and *It's Only Rock 'N' Roll* the riffs had fallen from the ringed fingers of Richards a little too easily, rarely rising beyond the prototype he'd created years earlier with 'Jumpin' Jack Flash'. On Black And Blue, Keith momentarily emerged from his cloud.

As with the entire album, the sound of 'Hand Of Fate' was crisp without seeming sterile, thanks to the work of engineers Glyn Johns, Keith Harwood and Phil McDonald. Each element, every drum beat and vocal line, was strong and unblemished through a staggering variety of rock blends, from funk to rock riffing to the reggae breeze of 'Cherry Oh Baby' to the wistful balladry of 'Memory Motel'.

After the superfunk of 'Hot Stuff', the Stones returned immediately to the land of the superhuman riff. Despite its vaguely spiritual tone, Jagger sings 'Hand Of Fate' as a man on the run after committing murder over the love of a woman.

Following a precedent set by the departed Mick Taylor, guitarist Wayne Perkins fires a jazzy rock lead across the band's charged rhythm. But 'Hand Of Fate' ultimately belongs to Keith.

"It doesn't matter about the B.B. Kings, Eric Claptons and Mick Taylors 'cause they do what they do. But I know they can't do what I do," Richards said later. "They can play as many notes under the sun but they just can't hold that rhythm down, baby… Everything I do is strongly based on rhythm 'cause that's what I'm best at. I've tried being a great guitar player, and – like Chuck Berry – I have failed."

MEMORY MOTEL

Richards leaves the guitar playing to Wayne Perkins and Harvey Mandel on 'Memory Motel', a story of endless, lonely nights on the road and of the good women met along the way. Jagger and Richards duet on the song in an often wounded tone, singing longingly for nights and memories long past.

Some memories are more intense than others. "I saw this girl pin Mick against a wall and try to take her clothes off on him," remembers percussionist Ollie E. Brown. "She just started undressing herself. Fans would scream, scratch, just like you see on TV. He just laughed."

Jagger and Richards sing across a lavish blend of keyboards: Mick on acoustic piano, Keith on electric piano, Preston on string synthesizer. Perkins strums an acoustic and Mandel plays electric, as Keith groans sagely, "She's got a mind of her own, and she uses it well."

As ever, sessions in Munich usually began in the evening and ended at sunrise. It would seem that Richards' rock muse only awoke after midnight. His night hours are spent with a guitar, not in bed. And songs often emerge from late-night jam sessions, as Ollie E. Brown discovered while touring with the Stones in the mid-seventies. "Keith would have an amplifier sent up to his room after a concert," Brown says. "Him and Woody might be sitting in the bedroom, noodling around; the next you know Mick walks in there and he might start singing to it. Then they might tape it for reference. The next thing you know you have a song."

HEY NEGRITA

That's Ron Wood's face on the back cover of *Black And Blue*, drifting in from stage left to a waiting world as the newest member of the Rolling Stones. His face is uncommonly proud and serious, clean-shaven and upright, even if the guitarist only plays on two album tracks here. They're enough. The first was Eric Johnson's quiet reggae song 'Cherry Oh Baby', but Wood's presence is most felt on 'Hey Negrita', which finds an appropriate voodoo groove within the scratchy, staccato guitars of Ron and Keith. Mick sings another lurid tale, this time shouting passionately of watching the street walkers before offering up one last dollar.

The song's Bayou rhythm was largely Wood's creation, erupting with twangy country-rock lines at the song's bridge. It was nothing that he couldn't have done with the Faces, but now it was in a different context, and the stakes were suddenly higher. Everything with the Stones was at a greater scale than anything Wood had known as a member of the Faces or, earlier, the Jeff Beck Group.

Wood sometimes asked his friend Bobby Womack for advice. "I remember him asking me, 'What do you think I should ask them? How much do you think

I should ask them for?' I said 'Man, I have no idea. Ask them for a million dollars,'" says Womack. "But they put him on a salary. He proved himself not only as being loyal, but with being a Stone they could count on."

Being a Stone has come at a price. In later years, Wood has managed to win songwriting credits from the Glimmer Twins. But the Rolling Stones would always focus first on the needs and desires of Jagger and Richards. The modern Stones were THEIR creation, THEIR personal venue, just as the Faces had been for Wood. With the Faces, at least, Wood had been the central musical force, crafting passages of passionate acoustic slide guitar and chunks of Stones-style rock to his own liking. Now he was part of the Stones machine, inevitably subverting his own musical voice. By the beginning of the 1980s even his solo recording career was essentially over.

But Wood came at another crucial time for the Stones. If *Black And Blue* represented a band finding renewed creative energy, then Wood was determined to keep the good vibes rolling. By 1978's *Some Girls*, young Ronnie was a key player within the band, a crucial presence that kept them together. And his raw, grinding guitar chunks locked in snugly with Keith's, just as if he'd been there all along.

"I certainly expect to contribute," Wood told *Rolling Stone* in 1977. "I've written a bit with Mick, a lot with Keith wherever we've been – New York, Paris, Munich – we've just collected all the ideas, like the stuff we were trying out in the studio. I've gotta make sure I do contribute. After all, I'd hate to become the dormant member of the Rolling Stones."

MELODY

Melody' was the only track recorded at the Rotterdam sessions to make it on to *Black And Blue*, and it's unlike anything else on the album. With an excited rush of horns arranged by Arif Mardin, it's an unlikely foray into jazz, with Charlie Watts on brushes. (Finally!) Mick stomps his feet, rolls his tongue, and sings a sloppy duet with Billy Preston. The song is warm and nasty, as Jagger struts through a sad, sad tale of a woman who spent all his money before falling into the arms of another man. "I'm looking for her high and low/like a mustard for a ham…"

The song slides across some spirited bar-room piano and soulful organ from Preston, who brings a measure of R&B into the mix. He joins Jagger for a lengthy session of joyful moaning, shuffling, groaning and scat singing at the track's end. During the 1970s, Preston enjoyed several hits of his own – 'Nothing From Nothing' and 'Will It Go Round In Circles', among others – enjoying the momentum of his work with the Beatles and the Stones. But none of it outclassed this stylish blend of jazz and blues.

FOOL TO CRY

For some listeners, the weepy ballad 'Fool To Cry' was even more disturbing than the strange dance-floor epic that had heralded the start of the album. This was music you expected from the Carpenters or Barry Manilow, NOT the Rolling Stones.

Jagger sings with rare vulnerability of being a father, a lover, a friend overcome with emotion and self-pity. It was not exactly rock and roll, but it was deeply effective, giving the Stones a top 10 hit in both Britain and America. "It's a fabulous song, and Jagger sings it brilliantly," Glyn Johns said later.

Johns had completed what he thought was the final mix of 'Fool To Cry' on December 4, 1974, only to see the band continue working and re-working the song when they returned to the studio after the Christmas break. The final version offers a slow blend of keyboards and guitars. Proof enough that even the most notorious of rock stars can master syrup if necessary.

CRAZY MAMA

Black And Blue closes with another straight-ahead Stones rocker, this time with Mick Jagger playing rhythm guitar, and Keith Richards firing off bits of country-funk lead. The talents of would-be sidemen Mandel, Perkins and Wood are not needed here, suggesting that Richards would have easily been up to the task alone if he'd wanted.

Recorded on March 29, 1975, 'Crazy Mama' is buoyed by layers of excited, dynamic guitar work. For Richards, who played guitar on Alexis Korner's *Get Off Of My Cloud* album of the same year, it may have been a simple exercise. But it was enough to reassure the fans that within the Rolling Stones, the slow decline had been at least temporarily halted. The blood was still boiling. And long may that continue.

DISCOGRAPHY

SINGLES

**Come On/I Want
To Be Loved**
June 1963
No. 20 in the UK
Decca/London Records

**I Wanna Be Your
Man/Stoned**
November 1963
No. 12 in the UK
Decca/London Records

**Not FadeAway/
Little By Little**
February 1964
No. 3 in the UK,
No. 48 in the US
Decca/London Records

**It's All Over Now/
Good Times, Bad
Times**
June 1964
No. 1 in the UK,
No. 26 in the US
Decca/London Records

**Tell Me (You're
Coming Back)/
I Just Wanna Make
Love To You**
August 1964
No. 24 in the US
Decca/London Records

**Time Is On My Side/
Congratulations**
November 1964
No. 6 in the US
Decca/London Records

**Little Red Rooster/
Off The Hook**
November 1964
No. 1 in the UK
Decca/London Records

**Heart Of Stone/
What A Shame**
January 1965
No. 19 in the US
Decca/London Records

**The Last Time/
Play With Fire**
February 1965
No. 1 in the UK,
No. 9 in the US
Decca/London Records

**(I Can't Get No)
Satisfaction/
Spider And The Fly**
August 1965
No 1 in both the
US and UK
Decca/London Records

**Get Off Of My
Cloud/
The Singer Not
The Song**
October 1965
No 1 in both the
US and UK
Decca/London Records

**As Tears Go By/
Gotta Get Away**
January 1966
No. 6 in the US
Decca/London Records

**19th Nervous
Breakdown/ As
Tears Go By**
February 1966
No. 1 in the US,
No. 2 in the UK
Decca/London Records

**Paint It Black/
Long Long While**
May 1966
No. 1 in both the
US and UK
Decca/London Records

**Have You Seen
Your Mother Baby,
Standing In The
Shadow?/Who's
Driving
Your Plane**
September 1966
No. 5 in the UK,
No. 9 in the US
Decca/London Records

**Let's Spend The
Night Together/
Ruby Tuesday**
January 1967
No. 1 in the US,
No. 3 in the UK
Decca/London Records

**We Love You/
Dandelion**
August 1967
No. 8 in the UK,
No. 14 in the US
Decca/London Records

**Jumping Jack Flash/
Child Of The Moon**
May 1968
No. 1 in the UK,
No. 3 in the US
Decca/London Records

**Honky Tonk
Women/
You Can't Always
Get What You Want**
July 1969
No 1 in both the
US and UK
Decca/London Records

**Brown Sugar/Bitch/
Let It Rock**
April 1971
No. 1 in the US,
No. 2 in the UK
Rolling Stones Records

**Tumbling Dice/
Sweet Black Angel**
April 1972
No. 7 in the US,
No. 5 in the UK
Rolling Stones Records

Angie/Silver Train
August 1973
No. 1 in the US,
No. 5 in the UK
Rolling Stones Records

**It's Only Rock 'N'
Roll/ Through The
Lonely Nights**
July 1974
No. 16 in the US,
No. 10 in the UK
Rolling Stones Records

**Fool To Cry/Crazy
Mama**
April 1976
No. 4 in the UK,
No. 10 in the US
Rolling Stones Records

**Miss You/Far Away
Eyes**
May 1978
No. 1 in the US,
No. 2 in the UK
Rolling Stones Records

**Beast Of Burden/
When The Whip
Comes Down**
August 1978
No. 8 in the US
Rolling Stones Records

**Respectable/
When The
Whip Comes
Down**
September 1978
No. 7 in the US,
No. 23 in the UK
Rolling Stones Records

**Emotional Rescue/
Down In The Hole**
July 1980
No. 3 in the US,
No. 9 in the UK
Rolling Stones Records

**She's So Cold/
Send It To Me**
September 1980
No. 26 in the US,
No. 33 in the UK
Rolling Stones Records

**Start Me Up/No
Use In Crying**
August 1981
No. 2 in the US,
No. 4 in the UK
Rolling Stones Records

**Waiting On
A Friend/
Little T & A**
November 1981
No. 13 in the US,
No. 50 in the UK
Rolling Stones Records

**Going To A Go-Go/
Beast of Burden**
May 1982
No. 25 in the US,
No. 26 in the UK
Rolling Stones Records

**Undercover Of The
Night/ All The Way
Down**
November 1983
No. 9 in the US,
No. 11 in the UK
Rolling Stones Records

**She Was Hot/
Think I'm Going
Mad**
February 1984
No. 42 in the UK,
No. 44 in the US
Rolling Stones Records

**Harlem Shuffle/Had
It With You**
March 1986
No. 5 in the US, No. 7
in the UK
Rolling Stones Records

**One Hit To The
Body/Fight**
May 1986
No. 28 in the US
Rolling Stones Records

**Mixed Emotions/
Fancyman Blues**
August 1989
No. 5 in the US,
No. 33 in the UK
Rolling Stones Records

**Rock And A
Hard Place**
November 1989
No. 23 in the US,
No. 63 in the UK
Rolling Stones Records

**Almost Hear
You Sigh/ Wish
I'd Never Met You**
June 1990
No. 31 in the UK,
No. 50 in the US
Rolling Stones Records

**Terrifying/Rock
And A Hard Place**
No. 82 in the UK
July 1990
Rolling Stones Records

**Highwire/2000 Light
Years From Home
(live)**
February 1991
No. 29 in the UK,
No. 57 in the US
Rolling Stones Records

Ruby Tuesday (live)
June 1991
No. 59 in the UK
Rolling Stones Records

**Love Is Strong/
The Storm**
July 1994.
No. 14 in the UK
No. 91 in the US
Rolling Stones
Records/Virgin

**You Got Me
Rocking/
Jump On Top Of Me**
October 1994
No. 23 in the UK
Rolling Stones
Records/Virgin

**Out Of Tears/Sparks
Will Fly**
November 1994
No. 36 in the UK
No. 60 in the US
Rolling Stones
Records/Virgin

**Like A Rolling
Stone/Black
Limousine**
October 1995
No. 12 in the UK
Rolling Stones
Records/Virgin

**Saint Of Me/Gimme
Shelter**
August 1998
No. 26 in the UK
No. 94 in the US
Rolling Stones
Records/Virgin

185

Don't Stop/Miss You (remix)
December 2002
No. 36 in the UK
Rolling Stones Records/Virgin

Streets of Love/ Rough Justice
August 2005
No. 15 in the UK
Rolling Stones Records/Virgin

Biggest Mistake/ Before They Make Me Run
August 2006
No. 51 in the UK
Rolling Stones Records/Virgin

Plundered My Soul/ All Down The Line
April 2010
Rolling Stones Records/Virgin

ALBUMS

Note that up until 1967's Between The Buttons, track listings varied greatly between the UK and the US.

The Rolling Stones
(England's Newest Hitmakers in the US)
April 1964
Route 66, I Just Want To Make Love To You, Honest I Do, I Need You Baby, Now I've Got A Witness, Little By Little, I'm A King Bee, Carol, Tell Me (You're Coming Back), Can I Get A Witness, You Can Make It If You Try, Walking The Dog
US 11, UK 1
ABCKO Records

12x5
(US-only release)
October 1964
Around And Around, Confessin' The Blues, Empty Heart, Time Is On My Side, Good Times, Bad Times, It's All Over Now, 2120 South Michigan Avenue, Under the Boardwalk, Congratulations, Grown Up Wrong, If You Need Me, Susie Q
US 3
London/ABKCO

The Rolling Stones No. 2
(UK-only release)
January 1965
Everybody Needs Somebody to Love, Down Home Girl, You Can't Catch Me, Time Is On My Side, What A Shame, Grown Up Wrong, Down The Road Apiece, Under the Boardwalk, I Can't Be Satisfied, Pain In My Heart, Off The Hook, Susie Q
UK 1
ABCKO Records

The Rolling Stones Now
(US-only release)
February 1965
Everybody Needs Somebody to Love, Down Home Girl, You Can't Catch Me, Heart Of Stone, What A Shame, I Need You Baby, Down The Road Apiece, Off The Hook, Pain In My Heart, Oh Baby (We Got A Good Thing Goin'), Little Red Rooster, Surprise, Surpise
US 5
London/ABKCO

Out Of Our Heads
September 1965
She Said Yeah, Mercy, Mercy, Hitch Hike, That's How Strong My Love Is, Good Times, Gotta Get Away, Talkin Bout You, Cry To Me, Oh Baby (We Got A Good Thing Goin'), Heart Of Stone, The Under Assistant West Coast Promotion Man, I'm Free
US 1, UK 2
ABCKO Records

Aftermath
April 1966
Mother's Little Helper, Stupid Girl, Lady Jane, Under My Thumb, Doncha Bother Me, Goin' Home, Flight 505, High And Dry, Out Of Time, It's Not Easy, I Am Waiting, Take It Or Leave It, Think, What To Do
US 1, UK 1
ABCKO Records

Between The Buttons
January 1967
Yesterday's Papers, My Obsession, Back Street Girl, Connection, She Smiled Sweetly, Cool, Calm And Collected, All Sold Out, Please Go Home, Who's Been Sleeping Here?, Complicated, Miss Amanda Jones, Something Happened To Me Yesterday
US 2, UK 3
ABCKO Records

Flowers
(US-only release)
June 1967
Ruby Tuesday, Have You Seen Your Mother, Baby, Standing in the Shadow?, Let's Spend The Night Together, Lady Jane, Out Of Time, My Girl, Back Street Girl, Please Go Home, Mother's Little Helper, Take It Or Leave It, Ride On Baby, Sittin' On A Fence
US 2
London/ABKCO

Their Satanic Majesties Request
December 1967
Sing This All Together, Citadel, In Another Land, 2000 Man, Sing This All Together (See What Happens), She's A Rainbow, The Lantern, Gomper, 2000 Light Years From Home, On With the Show
US 2, UK 3
ABCKO Records

Beggars Banquet
December 1968
Sympathy For The Devil, No Expectations, Dear Doctor, Parachute Woman, Jig-Saw Puzzle, Street Fighting Man, Prodigal Son, Stray Cat Blues, Factory Girl, Salt Of The Earth
US 2, UK 3
ABCKO Records

Let It Bleed
December 1969
Gimme Shelter, Love In Vain, Country Honk, Live With Me, Let It Bleed, Midnight Rambler, You Got the Silver, Monkey Man, You Can't Always Get What You Want
US 2, UK 1
ABCKO Records

Get Yer Ya Ya's Out*
September 1970
US 5, UK 1
ABCKO Records

Sticky Fingers
April 1971
Brown Sugar, Sway, Wild Horses, Can't You Hear Me Knocking, You Gotta Move, Bitch, I Got the Blues, Sister Morphine, Dead Flowers, Moonlight Mile
US 1, UK 1
Rolling Stones Records/Virgin

Exile On Main Street
May 1972
Rocks Off, Rip This Joint, Hip Shake, Casino Boogie, Tumbling Dice, Sweet Virginia, Torn And Frayed, Sweet Black Angel, Loving Cup, Happy, Turd On the Run, Ventilator Blues, Just Wanna See His Face, Let It Loose, All Down The Line, Stop Breaking Down, Shine A Light, Soul Survivor
US 1, UK 1
Rolling Stones Records/Virgin

Goats Head Soup
August 1973
Dancing With Mr D, 100 Years Ago, Coming Down Again, Doo Doo Doo Doo Doo (Heartbreaker), Angie, Silver Train, Hide Your Love, Winter, Can You Hear the Music, Star Star
US 1, UK 1
Rolling Stones Records/Virgin

It's Only Rock 'N' Roll
October 1974
If You Can't Rock Me, Ain't Too Proud To Beg, It's Only Rock 'N' Roll (But I Like It), Till The Next Goodbye, Time Waits For No One, Luxury, Dance Little Sister, If You Really Want To Be My Friend, Short And Curlies, Fingerprint File
US 1, UK 4
Rolling Stones Records/Virgin

Metamorphosis
June 1975
Out Of Time, Don't Lie To Me, Some Things Just Stick In Your Mind, Each And Every Day Of The Year, Heart Of Stone, I'd Much Rather Be With the Boys, (Walkin Thru The) Sleepy City, We're

Wastin' Time, Try A Little Harder, I Don't Know Why, If You Let Me, Jiving Sister Fanny, Downtown Suzie, Family, Memo From Turner, I'm Going Down
US 8
ABKCO

Black And Blue
April 1976
Hot Stuff, Hand Of Fate, Cherry Oh Baby, Memory Motel, Hey Negrita, Melody, Fool To Cry, Crazy Mama
US 1, UK 2
Rolling Stones Records/Virgin

Love You Live*
September 1977
US 5, UK 3
Rolling Stones Records/Virgin

Some Girls
June 1978
Miss You, When The Whip Comes Down, Just My Imagination, Some Girls, Lies, Far Away Eyes, Respectable, Before They Make Me Run, Beast Of Burden, Shattered
US 1, UK 2
Rolling Stones Records/Virgin

187

Emotional Rescue
June 1980
Dance (Pt. 1), Summer Romance, Send It To Me, Let Me Go, Indian Girl, Where The Boys Go, Down In The Hole, Emotional Rescue, She's So Cold, All About You
US 1, UK 1
Rolling Stones Records/Virgin

Tattoo You
September 1981
Start Me Up, Hang Fire, Slave, Little T&A, Black Limousine, Neighbors, Worried About You, Tops, Heaven, No Use In Crying, Waiting On A Friend
US 1, UK 1
Rolling Stones Records/Virgin

Still Life*
June 1982
UK. 2, US 20
Rolling Stones Records/Virgin

Undercover
November 1983
Undercover Of The Night, She Was Hot, Tie You Up (The Pain Of Love), Wanna Hold You, Feel On Baby, Too Much Blood, Pretty Beat Up, Too Tough, All The Way Down, It Must Be Hell
UK 1, US 4
Rolling Stones Records/Virgin

Dirty Work
April 1986
One Hit (To The Body), Fight, Harlem Shuffle, Hold Back, Too Rude, Winning Ugly, Back To Zero, Dirty Work, Had It With You, Sleep Tonight
US 4, UK 3
Rolling Stones Records/Virgin

Steel Wheels
September 1989
Sad Sad Sad, Mixed Emotions, Terrifying, Hold On To Your Hat, Hearts For Sale, Blinded By Love, Rock And A Hard Place, Can't Be Seen, Almost Hear You Sigh, Continental Drift, Break The Spell, Slipping Away
US 3, UK 2
Rolling Stones Records/Virgin

Flashpoint *
April 1991
UK 6
Rolling Stones Records/Virgin

Voodoo Lounge
August 1994
Love Is Strong, You Got Me Rocking, Sparks Will Fly, The Worst, News Faces, Moon Is Up, Out of Tears, I Go Wild, Brand New Car, Sweethearts

Together, Suck On The Jugular, Blinded By Rainbows, Baby Break It Down, Thru And Thru, Mean Disposition
US 2, UK 2
Rolling Stones Records/Virgin

Stripped*
(May 1995)
Rolling Stones Records/Virgin

The Rolling Stones Rock And Roll Circus
October 1995
1968 film Including performances of Jumping Jack Flash, Parachute Woman, No Expectations, You Can't Always Get What You Want, Sympathy For The Devil, Salt Of The Earth ABKCO Records New release (as yet untitled) (October 1997) Thief In The Night, Out of Control, Juiced, Saint, Already Over Me, Always Suffering, Nobody's Seen My Baby, Gin Face, Too Tight, You Don't Have to Mean It, How Can I Stop, Flip The Switch, Anyway You Look At It
Rolling Stones Records/Virgin

Bridges To Babylon
September 1997
Flip The Switch, Anybody Seen My Baby?, Low Down, Already Over Me, Gunface, You Don't Have To Mean It, Out of Control, Saint Of Me, Might As Well Get Juiced, Always Suffering, Too Tight, Thief In The Night, How Can I Stop?
US 2, UK 6
Rolling Stones Records/Virgin

No Security*
November 1998
US 34, UK 67
Rolling Stones Records/Virgin

Live Licks*
November 2004
US 50, UK 38

A Bigger Bang
September 2005
Rough Justice, Let Me Down Slow, It Won't Take Long, Rain Fall Down, Streets Of Love, Back Of My Hand, She Saw Me Coming, Biggest Mistake, This Place Is Empty, "Oh No, Not You Again, Dangerous Beauty, Laugh, I Nearly Died, Sweet Neo Con, Look What The Cat Dragged In, Driving Too Fast, Infamy

US 3, UK 2
Rolling Stones
Records/Virgin

Shine A Light
April, 2008
Jumpin' Jack Flash,
Shattered, She Was
Hot, All Down the
Line, Loving Cup, As
Tears Go By, Some
Girls, Just My
Imagination, Far Away
Eyes, Champagne &
Reefer, Tumbling Dice,
Band introductions,
You Got the Silve,
Connection, Martin
Scorsese intro,
Sympathy for the
Devil, Live with Me,
Start Me Up, Brown
Sugar, (I Can't Get
No) Satisfaction, Paint
It Black, Little T&A,
I'm Free, Shine a Light
US 11, UK 2

**Entries marked with
an asterisk denote
live albums.**

EPS

The Rolling Stones
January 1964
Bye Bye Johnny,
Money, You Better
Move On, Poison Ivy
Decca/London

Five By Five
August 1964
If You Need Me,
Empty Heart, 2120
South Michigan

Avenue, Confessin'
The Blues, Around
And Around
Decca/London

**Got Live If You
Want It**
June 1965
We Want the Stones,
Everybody Needs
Somebody To Love,
Pain In My Heart,
(Get Your Kicks On)
Route 66, I'm Moving
On, I'm Alright
ABKCO Records

COMPILATIONS

**There have been
numerous Rolling
Stones compilations
produced over the
past 45 years. This
is a selection of the
better collections.**

**Big Hits (High
Tide And
Green Grass)**
November 1966
US 2, UK 4
ABKCO Records

**Through The Past
Darkly**
(Big Hits Volume 2)
September 1969
US 2, UK 1
ABKCO Records

Stone Age
April 1971
UK 5
ABKCO Records

Made In The Shade
June 1975
US 6, UK 10
Rolling Stones Records

**Sucking In The
Seventies**
May 1981
Shattered, Everything
Is Turning To Gold,
Hot Stuff, Time Waits
For No One, Fool To
Cry, Mannish Boy,
When The Whip
Comes Down, If I Was
A Dancer (Dance Pt.
2), Crazy Mama, Beast
of Burden
US 17
Rolling Stones Records
Singles Collection:
The London Years
September 1989
ABKCO Records

Rewind (1971–1984)
November 1989
Rolling Stones
Records/Virgin

**Jump Back (The
Best Of...)**
November 1993
ABKCO Records

Forty Licks
September 2002
US 2, UK2
Virgin/ABKCO/Decca

Rarities 1971-2003
August 2004
US 76
Rolling Stones
Records/Virgin

**Rolled Gold: The
Very Best Of The
Rolling Stones**
November 2007
UK 26
Rolling Stones
Records/Virgin

INDEX

The publishers would like to thank the following sources for their kind permission to reproduce the pictures in this book:

Corbis: Bettmann: 11, 19, 22, 27, 47, 52, 59, 89, 98, 114, 127, 136, 141; /Hulton-Deutsch Collection: 38, 87, 109, 119

Getty Images: 17; /Redferns: 68, 125, 165

London Features International: 30, 32, 66, 115, 123, 134, 146, 153; / Michael Putland: 158, 171, 178

Pictorial Press Ltd. 2, 6, 12, 25, 35, 42, 55, 57, 63, 65, 73, 79, 83, 90, 95, 97, 100, 103, 106, 111, 129, 133, 138, 148, 151, 160, 177, 181

Retna Pictures Ltd.: 3; /Michael Putland: 93; /G.Hanekroot/Sunshine: 8, 167, 174

Every effort has been made to acknowledge correctly and contact the source and/or copyright holder of each picture, and Carlton Books Limited apologises for any unintentional errors, or omissions which will be corrected in future editions of this book.